PEOPLE AT WORK
a practical guide to organizational change

by

Dave Francis
Mike Woodcock

University Associates, Inc.
7596 Eads Avenue
La Jolla, California 92037

foreword

Instead of inviting a famous person to write a foreword, we decided we would rather have the opinion of a practicing manager who is neither an eminent tycoon nor a pundit.

We therefore invited a successful manager of a small company to read the book and tell us what she thought. Because her "people problems" are real, her opinion is much more valuable to us.

It was very easy to understand, which to me is most important. Quite a few of the books I have bought in the past would be useful if you had worked your way up in a large organisation and had the experience first. Very few writers seem to cater for managers of firms with limited knowledge and experience; mostly we learn by mistakes which, whilst well remembered, are costly. I think we could have avoided a few on the way if books like this had been available in language which everyone understands.

Sheila Mercer, manager of Carlsbro Sound Equipment,
a small British firm that makes high-quality sound equipment
for pop groups and specialized users

If you dig very deeply into
any problem, you will get to "people."
J. Watson Wilson

preface

In our public library there are several shelves packed with books that purport to teach managers how to run their businesses more effectively. There are so many books, articles, films, courses, consultants, and improvement systems available that it is quite clear that a manager who wanted to understand all the theory would have no time left to manage anything at all.

We believe that we can justify adding another book to the pile, because *People at Work* is not another version of orthodox management theory. Developed in England, this book, we believe, is equally applicable in its ideas, experiences, and methods to managers everywhere.

We write, first, for those who manage and, second, for those who teach management practice. Our experience is largely in industry and business, but the ideas and methods described in this book can also clearly be used in noncommercial organizations. So, whether you run an animal shelter, a hospital, or the local dramatics club, there is no reason why the book is any less relevant.

When we began writing this book, we first wrote down our own principles to guide us. We would like to share them with you because they underlie all the ideas in the book.

First and foremost, we wanted to write a book that would be practical and useful to those who actually manage, a book that combines academic knowledge and a practical approach. This means that *People at Work* will not offer you elaborate theory and research. Instead, we hope you will enjoy reading it and will use it as a source of ideas in your own organization.

Secondly, we wanted to describe only those practices that we have actually witnessed as being successful in real situations. The book, like a collection of traveller's tales, pulls together ideas and experiences from a variety of companies and individuals.

The third principle that largely determines the shape of this book is our belief that development comes primarily from personal experience. Accordingly, although an idea may be understood theoretically, it is unlikely to have any real effect until put to the test. We invite you to explore for yourself your own particular situation; most of the book is devoted to ways of doing just this.

If you ask a manager about his job he is likely to say something like this: "Successful management is seeing opportunities and making constructive things happen despite difficulties." Managers would be drones if everything were straightforward and predictable. There are challenges, threats, and uncertainties in many organizational situations. Successful managers learn to cope creatively with difficulties and to make good use of the resources available.

A resource is "a source of strength," and each of us has particular strengths. Development is learning to use these strengths effectively. We often see in others, and experience for ourselves, just how difficult it is to achieve real development. Organizations that do not set out to help people develop find it very difficult to avoid cozy routines and general frustration. All too often procedures replace thought, status symbols replace ability, and new ideas become acceptable only if they are in the right-colored box.

It is people who provide the creative element of an operation and make it really swing or flop. *People at Work* tells how to channel more of the latent strengths in people to benefit both the individuals concerned and the organization for which they work.

Anyone who has tried to make major improvements in an organization knows that the process is frequently difficult and demanding. As you read through the book, you will find sufficient ideas to work with seriously for many months. Experience shows us that there is no sense in trying to do too much too soon, and we ask you to do only what you feel is relevant and can be reasonably accomplished. However, when you do decide to try an idea or an activity, make a resolution to tackle it seriously, giving the time and priority necessary to do a proper job and applying the quality standards you use for your own product or service.

ACKNOWLEDGEMENTS

The ideas and methods we describe come from far too many sources to acknowledge each one separately, and we owe an enormous debt to all of the researchers, writers, and trainers who have mapped out this field before us. We especially wish to thank our colleagues at the Food, Drink and Tobacco Industry Training Board, and the dozens of companies that have shared their experiences with us. We hope, in return, that those who have contributed to the book will be able to enjoy it and profit from it.

To some writers and teachers, who have been especially important to us, we owe a particular debt. We were helped by Abraham Maslow to understand the idea of blockages. Jackie Doyle, Barry Goodfield, Tony Blake, Stan Herman, Lynam Ketcham, and Roger Harrison helped us to realize the value of a Gestalt approach to development. We are also indebted to Rensis Likert, Chris Argyris, Frederick Herzberg, Bill Pfeiffer, and Ted Matchett, each of whom contributed something of great value. We also express our thanks to Bert Medlam, Production Manager at General Foods, Ltd., U. K., whose practical insight helped fit many things together.

Part of the structure of this book was inspired by an exceptionally interesting training approach developed by Dr. E. R. Danzig and Dr. E. C. Nevis called "Blocks to Creativity."

Additionally, we are indebted to those who read and commented on earlier drafts, including Terry Wilson, Walter Oakey, John Frank, Peter Sperring, David Dennington, Ron Johnson, and Sheila Mercer.

Finally, a big thank you to Josie Marriott, our typist, who made sense out of misspelt copy and confusing scraps of paper, and to our tireless editors, Deborah Osborn and Marion Fusco.

Of course, responsibility for all errors, inadequacies, and stupidities is ours alone.

To improve later editions of this book, we are interested in your suggestions and methods, and we would be delighted to know about your experiences. Please write to us in care of our publishers. We hope that you find *People at Work* a wealth of practical ideas.

Nottingham, England   Dave Francis
May, 1975   Mike Woodcock

contents

part one

Introduction to Principles

How to Use PEOPLE AT WORK

Most books are intended to be read, digested, and analyzed. This one is different. It is meant to be a practical guide to help you develop a more effective organization. Later you will find dozens of ideas that you can use, develop, expand, and adapt for yourself.

Although the book's four parts follow a logical sequence, the chapters can be used in any order you like. Set up more like a meal at a cafeteria than a four-course luncheon, the book lets you dip in wherever you wish, choose what most appeals to you, and work from there.

PLAN OF THE BOOK

Part One introduces the book, describes "people problems," and then outlines at what stages in the development of a typical organization people problems are likely to occur.

Part Two—Taking Your Organization's Temperature—is unusual, but we hope that you will find it useful and revealing. We have developed a questionnaire to help you clarify which areas of your business are most in need of development. This is not a test because there are no "right" answers; it is simply a way of helping you identify which kinds of people problems need to be investigated, understood, and solved. We have called these problems *blockages*. They all have this characteristic: a blockage prevents people from putting their intelligence, energy, and effort to productive use. Research in all areas of business and with all sizes of firms has shown us that most difficulties can be described under these eleven blockages. The blockages have the same effect on companies as they do on pipes and drains: they cut down the proper flow between one part and another, thereby decreasing the efficiency of the system as a whole.

We believe that discovering and clearing the blockages in your organization is the most practical and effective way to improve the contribution of people. The most important and difficult step in accomplishing this is deciding what your blockages actually look like and determining what effect they have.

Blockages will not disappear simply because you want them to vanish; rather, they must become known and understood—"know thine enemy." Once the enemy is known, it becomes much more vulnerable to being vanquished. It is the same with organization blockages: get to know them well; they are part of you, and once they are accepted you will have a much better chance of dealing with them.

Completing the questionnaire in Part Two will give you a rating on each of the eleven blockages that may be affecting your organization. You can then explore and work on the most serious and relevant ones in greater depth. Your assessment will become even more valid if you ask other people in the organization to fill out the same questionnaire, thereby enabling you to compare different perceptions of what needs to be done.

Part Three is a series of eleven short essays, each of which gives greater detail about the typical nature of one blockage. By choosing the essays that seem most relevant to you, you can work on the blockages that are causing the most problems at the moment and that you would be prepared to invest time, effort, and perhaps money in relieving. At the end of each essay we list activities that will enable you to explore more carefully the nature and possible solution of the particular blockage.

Part Four collects the ideas and activities for all the blockages. By working through them, you will find that the issues become clearer and it becomes easier to make constructive changes. In a few cases, the activities may seem somewhat unusual at first; yet they have proven to be useful to managers.

Trying an activity for yourself will involve a certain amount of time and perhaps a small risk, but the attempt should also be interesting, revealing, and enjoyable. You will probably find, as we have done, that the activities frequently give more than they appear to offer.

An **Appendix** provides more ideas about how to use outside resources for further help, in the event that you may want to learn more or get some additional assistance. There are a great many people who claim that they can help you. Our experience indicates that careful discrimination is needed in selecting "outside" assistance.

RELEVANCE OF THE IDEAS IN People at Work

You should find the ideas in this book useful in improving your effectiveness and in planning your future. It is often helpful to consider which of the blockages is most relevant to you as an individual.

Take the case of one manager we know. Polished and efficient, he was appointed head of external communication and customer service in an international organization. Soon systems were installed and decisions were made with an efficiency that was held up as an example to others. But good people began to leave, and dullards got the influential jobs. The output of his department became tedious and superficial. Privately, people admitted that they were scared of the manager's outspoken and inexorable logic. He saw creativity as upsetting the beauty of the machine; people did not dare to be innovative outside of his very narrow limits. Hence, this manager, who was so strong on conventional management control, was unable to build a truly creative climate. For him, development meant working on this blockage. For a different individual, however, exactly the opposite may have been the case.

A Team Approach

We have found that our ideas, although relevant to individuals, gain immeasurably when used as the basis for a team approach. If you feel it is possible to involve your colleagues, the following plan suggests a method to help you get started.

First, you need to consider our ideas and see whether you agree with them. If you do not feel comfortable and "at home" with our views, then there is no point in proceeding. Please examine how you are feeling while you read. You may find yourself agreeing with our suggestions and experiences, or there may be something that you would like to accept but really do not believe.

Therefore, your first step is to decide whether the book is in agreement with your own views. When you have satisfied yourself that our direction is one in which you would like to travel, ask for the views of a few colleagues in your firm whose opinions you value. See whether the book excites and interests them, or, to use a current expression, "turns them on."

Since the will to proceed can evaporate quickly, one way to progress is to form a steering committee. As it is more likely to be successful if it is as widely representative as possible, it should first investigate its own views about the ideas in the book. A useful step in accomplishing this is for the committee to write a specific statement of the principles it would like to see employed in the management of people in the organization. Once this "statement of interest" has been prepared, it is best to work on some activities as soon as possible. The energy for change will result only from practical efforts which help people see things differently.

A Few Tips to Increase Your Chances of Success

We have seen many individuals, organizations, and groups try the ideas in this book. Sometimes genuine improvement has resulted, but on other occasions it has been like pouring sour cream into coffee. There are no hard and fast rules to success, but these tips, which we have discovered through bitter experience, can greatly improve your chances of useful results.

Tip 1

Consult widely and genuinely to collect ideas and views. This is important for three reasons:

(1) People really do have useful contributions to make that will improve the quality of any work.

(2) By being consulted, people will feel more committed to any project.

(3) By using people's talents more widely, you are putting into practice the principles that underlie *People at Work*.

It is easy to look upon consultation as a chore or as a subtle way of selling an idea. Managers frequently become highly skilled at forcing their ideas on others. Such manipulation, however, will undermine the whole effort.

Tip 2

Work seriously and methodically toward putting the ideas into practice.

Every manager is more serious about some aspects of his work than he is about others. It may be, for example, that production planning or cost control is given maximum attention while everything else comes second. The changes for which you aim will require much care from the managers involved, and adequate time and other resources are essential. Only through actual implementation of ideas can meaningful development occur.

Tip 3

Start with modest objectives.

Many schemes fail because they are too extensive, and managers do not have the time, skills, or patience to see them through. It is invariably better to begin with a topic that can be grasped and handled by the people concerned. This way, results can be seen relatively quickly, and the amount of effort required is not felt to be excessive.

In addition, the management team builds experience in handling projects and becomes increasingly prepared and able to deal with more intractable problems.

Tip 4

Encourage frequent and frank discussions about principles and practices.

To achieve real benefits, all those involved need to reconsider fundamental views that may well have become an unexamined part of their way of life. Such views change only if they are opened and explored at length and in a constructive atmosphere. Managers need to become accustomed to discussing matters of principle with their colleagues. These may include commercial objectives, but discussion needs to be more widely based. Such questions as democracy in the organization and the responsibility of a company to the community are matters that need to be thoroughly considered.

Tip 5

Decide what you want to achieve and how to measure success or the lack of it.

This has probably been said a million times, but it is rarely done. Well-thought-out objectives help make any operation much clearer and more effective. Clarity and agreement about purpose and aim give a much greater feeling of sanity and meaning. By determining objectives you will be better able to review the value of your efforts and make even better plans for the future.

DEVELOPMENT STYLES

People approach change in different ways. Some, the "dilettantes," involve themselves in random activities only in a superficial way, never becoming truly motivated or involved. Others, the inhibited, refuse to take risks; they avoid all uncertainties, preferring to remain introspective and aloof rather than to face new challenges. Between these two extremes are the dreamers, involved in their imaginations only, preferring to create perfection in their heads rather than to build a better real world; and the discontented, always vainly seeking a magic formula that they hope will transform everything without personal effort.

None of these types achieve truly constructive and meaningful change:

the dilettantes   —because they taste everything but never persist.

the inhibited   —because they are never willing to explore anything unknown and different.

the dreamers   —because their imagination and fine words satisfy
their need for change while actually accom-
plishing little.

the discontented —because they are always hoping to find the magic
formula that will bring perfection, and they
do not realize that real effort on their part is
necessary.

Our personal experience proves that although it is hard to avoid
all the traps—and we fail to achieve our goals time and time again—
it is invariably better to experiment and adventure than to stagnate.
Things do not stand still. There is a saying that "where there is no evo-
lution, there is degeneration."

Defining People Problems

Managing people is a strange and uniquely difficult job. All sorts of difficulties and dilemmas may crop up, and frequently no clear way out can be seen. Any experienced manager is able to talk for hours about the difficulties he has faced with his people, yet he should also be able to talk about the positive side. People often give immense loyalty and effort to their employers, going far beyond the essential requirements of the job. Managers and subordinates may also form deep, gratifying friendships.

All organizations have people problems of one sort or another. Sometimes these problems are so serious that the organization becomes unprofitable, but usually they are not disastrous, and just act as a ball and chain to inhibit progress.

Listing all the various types of people problems that can face managers would reveal an excessively gloomy picture; most likely, however, you will not recognize all of them in your organization.

TYPICAL PEOPLE PROBLEMS

People problems frequently seem to begin with the wrong person in a job. Almost every organization has its share of misfits, cranks, and half-wits. Joe is too dim, slow, and rude, whereas Mary is excessively flighty and inaccurate. And so it goes. Managers feel stuck with people that they never would have hired had they known the final outcome.

Another frequent grumble concerns organizational "red tape." People usually feel powerless against the organization and often react as if they were caught in a thunderstorm on a summer afternoon—they run for cover and hope that the disturbance will go away. A poorly designed organization stunts progress and makes inefficiency inevitable. It is well worth the time and trouble to alleviate the situation.

We all know the manager who acts as if he were trying to steer an ocean liner by dangling an oar into the sea; somehow the ship sails onward, but no one is really in command. The concept of "control" is one of the most fascinating aspects of management. Inadequate control results in confusion, apathy, and decadence; yet excessive control results in fascism, fear, and rebellion. There is no absolute way to know what kind of control is appropriate in a given circumstance; much depends on the individual situation. At the center of the problem is the mechanism for creating and channelling information. Nothing is more revealing about a company than discovering who really makes the decisions. Often there are a lot of surprises!

Another manager's protest is that new people take too long to learn a job in the first place, and subsequently fail to keep their skills current. Employees often leave before they actually become useful; older technicians, craftsmen, professional workers, and managers frequently work with concepts that are twenty years out of date. There are a host of inefficiencies and added costs, including wasted materials, lost opportunities, training instructors' time, and, with senior people, outdated professional practices, that affect a company's competitive position.

Getting people to work is one thing, but getting them to work for the direct interest of the organization is quite another. We know of a small engineering factory where the craftsmen spend most of the day as solemn as deacons and twice as slow; but they spring to life at lunch time to make parts for their cars, lawn mowers, and children's toys. One-half mile away, a manager of a group of computer-systems analysts noticed that his men had stopped taking thirty-minute coffee breaks and seemed to be working assiduously on new programs. At first he attributed this to his motivational talks, but he discovered, quite by accident, that the analysts were developing a computerized betting method that should provide them with extraordinary wins on the horses.

When a manager finds his people putting real effort into the needs of the business, he can feel proud of a major achievement.

All companies must develop new ideas and products to live, and genuine creative work is as essential as the annual balance sheet. Managers often find that the suggestion box contains ideas that would send the managing supervisor directly to the hospital if taken seriously; and senior management often bemoans the "lack of initiative" of the junior staff. Somehow, other companies always seem to have the good ideas a bit faster and to capitalize on them more effectively.

Organizations exist to do jobs that a single individual cannot handle alone. Often, however, people seem to pull in separate directions just as much as they try to pull together. Management meetings are a case in point. Although, on the surface, a civilized attitude prevails, underneath jungle fighting, one-upmanship, defensiveness, muddle-headed thinking, and sheer maliciousness are often in control. Important matters are rarely debated or even confronted because they are too sensitive, complicated, or intimidating. Group members may lack the mental skills to come to grips with difficult problems, or, following Parkinson's Law, they may spend more time discussing the purchase of a new coffee machine than the key investment decision of the year.

All of us make thousands of choices every day about the way we behave in all sorts of situations, although we almost never give the matter a moment's thought. These judgments about suitable behavior are extremely important in determining the quality and character of our lives. Managers, as well as members of other groups, tend to develop a collective way of seeing the world. Although difficult to observe through isolated incidents, these shared values underlie all their actions.

At the root of this problem is the concept of authority. In many countries, the ready acceptance of traditional authority is being increasingly questioned. Often, authority and power are hated and feared because of their frequent misuse. Managers who treat people as units of labor to be restricted and kept under tight discipline find that the people so managed respond in predictable ways: they tend to feel little personal identification with the business and to seek an outlet for their unused energies—perhaps in leisure or in militant attitudes and subversion at work. Managers and management groups frequently work from principles that have the effect of creating anger, boredom, and apathy in their employees.

We frequently find companies in a high state of panic because a key job has become vacant and no one is around to fill the slot. In desperation, managers have urgent meetings until someone is finally selected as the best of a bad lot. For a reason we cannot determine, managers often think it unethical to plan the people requirements of the business in years to come. Many companies have lost golden opportunities because of the lack of skilled people at the right time, and there must be thousands of managers sadly contemplating how much better the business would be if a crisis decision had not saddled the company with Mr. Snidvong's inept and morose managerial style.

It is much easier to write books about defining objectives than to deal with them in business. All of the uncertainties in the market and in the environment make the job of clarifying the aims of business subtle and complex, yet the job must be done and company aims frequently revised. Failure can lead to a peculiar business malaise that takes root and, like a virile germ, pollutes the organization. The illness has one main symptom—people forget the real purpose of their work and perform in a fragmented, half-hearted, or misguided way.

Finally we come to the embarrassing question of money. Psychological satisfactions are food for the spirit but not meat for the body; hence, we find that ceaseless haggling over wage rates and rewards is the soap opera of many organizations. Yet, the most tangible measure of a person's contribution and value is his remuneration.

Pavlov showed us that dogs will learn all manner of unusual behaviors if rewarded in certain ways, and observation shows us that people in organizations are affected far more than they realize by the reward system. The most widespread people malaises focus around issues of payment, because in this way people are weighed, measured, assessed, and categorized.

It would be wonderfully tidy if managers capable of dealing with all these problems could be manufactured like tubs of margarine—just put in the ingredients at one end, carry out certain processes, and out pops the finished product to the required standard. Unfortunately, however, despite the ambitions of clever personnel experts, there is no foolproof way of developing managers. Some of the most highly trained people simply develop more skilled ways of being incompetent. Nevertheless, much can be done to provide managers with opportunities to develop their own capacity to handle problems creatively. When this is neglected, the organization usually lacks people with the breadth of vision, clarity of purpose, and depth of understanding to handle problems competently.

ELEVEN COMMON BLOCKAGES

As you have read through these last pages, you may have recognized various situations with which you have suffered in the past or are wrestling with at this moment. All of the problems and difficulties we have described are, basically, *people problems,* which can be seen as organization blockages that decrease the efficiency of the system as a whole. Almost all of these can be described under the following headings.

Blockage 1. Inadequate Recruitment and Selection—The people being hired lack the knowledge, personality, or skills appropriate to the organization's needs.

Blockage 2. Confused Organizational Structure—The way in which people are organized is wasteful or inefficient.

Blockage 3. Inadequate Control—Poor decisions are made because of faulty information in the hands of inappropriate people.

Blockage 4. Poor Training—People are not learning efficiently to do things that would materially improve their performance.

Blockage 5. Low Motivation—People do not feel greatly concerned about the organization and are not willing to expend much effort to further common goals.

Blockage 6. Low Creativity—Good ideas for improvement are not being properly put to use, so stagnation occurs.

Blockage 7. Poor Teamwork—People who should be contributing to common tasks either do not wish to work together or find that there are too many obstacles to do so.

Blockage 8. Inappropriate Management Philosophy—Conscious and unconscious management principles that underlie decisions and create the atmosphere are unrealistic or inhumane.

Blockage 9. Lack of Succession Planning and Management Development—Sufficient preparation for important future job vacancies is not being undertaken.

Blockage 10. Unclear Aims—The reasons for doing things are either muddy or badly explained.

Blockage 11. Unfair Rewards—People are not rewarded in ways that satisfy them, or the reward system works against the health of the organization.

Your organization may have more trouble with some of these blockages than others. The aim is to determine which blockages are hurting you the most and to proceed to clear them.

Communication as a Blockage

Notice that, although every one of our blockages has a great deal to do with communication, we decided not to deal with this as a separate topic. Poor communication is the result of a deeper malaise and cannot be fundamentally improved without treating the causes. Working on clearing the blockages we describe is an exercise in communication in its own right.

DEFINING A HEALTHY ORGANIZATION

To conclude this chapter, we will describe how a really healthy people system looks. Perhaps a badge saying *I've unblocked our people system* should be issued to chief executives who can honestly say that the following eleven points describe their companies.

A company without blockages has the following characteristics:

1. Appropriate people are selected who can handle the requirements of the job and grow with the firm.

2. The organizational framework enables and encourages work to be done; it does not prevent it.

3. Control is clearly in the hands of the most appropriate people who get the necessary information to make their decisions.

4. People have the facilities to learn quickly what they need to know to be "on top" of their jobs.

5. Those who work in the firm want it to flourish and are prepared to put effort into making this happen.

6. Sufficient, good, new ideas are initiated and implemented to keep the firm ahead in its field.

7. People who need to work together find that the experience is constructive, enjoyable, and relatively open.

8. Managers take their responsibilities seriously and test the soundness of their beliefs by what happens in practice.

9. Important future staffing needs are identified and prepared for in good time, and a sufficiently large pool of potential management talent is created.

10. The organization knows where it wants to go and why it wants to go there.

11. Those who make the largest contribution to the health of the enterprise get the highest rewards, and the payment system is generally felt to be just and equitable.

The Developing Organization

HOW ORGANIZATIONS DEVELOP

Companies often begin with an idea and a person with the strength and the vision to build a business. Although many enterprises fail in the early days when there are numerous setbacks and difficulties, a few take root and grow. The head of a young business, often a person of energy and drive, selects his staff with considerable care, frequently from his personal friends. Together they form a great team, working well as a close group, finding challenges and defeating problems.

Increasingly, today, a large company will establish a new venture from scratch. The new operation will have the challenge and excitement that come with innovation and yet have professional management and capital reserves from the parent company. The vigor of a young organization often encourages an exceptional commitment from people. We know a new company producing 20 percent more of the same product than its middle-aged parent across the road because of the additional energy that a new organization can harness.

As a business gets larger, it becomes impossible for its originator to plan, coordinate, and control operations, while still providing the firm with the vital energy it needs to keep alive. Time after time this is a period of profound confusion. In a family firm, it often coincides with the transfer of management to members of the second generation, who frequently lack the knowledge, personal relationships, and drive of the founder.

The way through this "profound confusion" is by employing professional management principles. It may take a few years, but then information and control systems begin to replace off-the-cuff decisions. New people are hired after objective selection, rather than from personal friends. Jobs are measured and specified, instead of being determined by the persons who hold them. Marketing, finance, production planning and control, transportation, training, buying, and other functions proliferate and become separate units. Management may then try to overcome fragmentation by some form of unified procedure like "Management by Objectives."

While each of these developments adds something of real value to an organization, there is a scorpion's sting in the tail. After a while, it becomes a massive task just to keep all the elements going down the same road. The system becomes so unwieldy and ponderous that it reacts slowly and clumsily to new circumstances. This is compounded by another striking feature—employees increasingly forget the purpose of their jobs and lose interest in working positively for the company. When this happens, the system becomes an almost impenetrable obstacle to be fought while one has the energy. It is a paradox that the very ideas and systems that helped bring the company out of confusion can become a heavy, smothering web of red tape.

This leads to a second period of upheaval, confusion, and ineffectiveness. In a way, the company is suffering from middle age, and it can either rejuvenate itself or grow old in its systems, rigidities, and tired disillusions. At this stage, it is necessary to find the energy and clarity of purpose that were so characteristic in the company's early years, without losing the positive value of modern management principles. This time-consuming and fundamental task becomes a permanent part of the organization's way of life.

Purpose and Effectiveness

These two questions are of real and central importance to the later development of an organization: "What are our purposes?" and "How can we organize work most effectively?" Only when these two questions are genuinely evaluated throughout the organization can it develop into a really healthy and productive company.

With some variations, this process has been seen in organizations all over the world. One point is clear: the problems that affect an organization at one stage in its growth are fundamentally different from those at another stage; therefore, no single solution can be applied in every case.

Managers can be helped by understanding how organizations are formed, grow older, mature, and often degenerate. There is, however, no reason why an organization must die. The strong forces that bring about decay can be countered by preventing blind tradition from becoming the master of circumstances.

Some of the activities presented in Part Four will help you see your present stage of development and clarify the steps needed to effect change.

HOW CHANGE OCCURS

We all would like change to be planned, tidy, and undemanding; but in actual life, real development is frequently confused, untidy, and difficult. In this situation, it is helpful to know that one is not alone, that everyone confronts the same dilemma. Individually and organizationally, development occurs by learning how to work positively with difficulties, confusion, and circumstances.

Many people work quite hard and put in long hours to do the best job they can. Often they do not see many practical ways of improving the situation, either because they have tried everything they know, or because they feel that there are too many obstacles in the way. Frequently, though, the limitations are as much in people themselves as in the situation.

It is easy for management pundits to give advice, but unless something is experienced by an individual as a need or a requirement, it is unlikely that change will occur. During World War II, housewives were lectured that they could contribute to the war effort by serving unpopular cuts of meat to their families. Only a small proportion of the women present took the advice because they were not personally committed to action. When a similar group of women participated in an open discussion, however, many more actually cooked the dishes in their own kitchens because the discussion aroused their personal commitment. Thus, a need for change must be felt by a person before there is much of a possibility that something will actually be done.

Development also requires having a mental picture of how things will look when they are better. We need to visualize the final objective in terms that make sense to us, so that plans can be made to move in one direction or another. Sometimes a long-range view is not possible, thus increasing the need for a broad perspective to guide our view of the immediate future. The following example may help make the process clearer.

Mr. Giant, forty pounds overweight, is flabby in all the places where it is possible to be flabby. He has not exercised regularly for years, with the possible exception of developing his arm at the local bar. He avoids climbing stairs as a cat avoids water. One morning he wakes up, faces his mirror, and decides that he wants to be fit. He has made this decision often in the past, but his will usually cracks at the first pang of hunger or ache of an unused muscle. But this time he is serious. In order to accomplish his goal, he needs to visualize the improvements he wants to achieve. Experience tells us that the more clearly he is able to visualize the end product, the more likely it is that he will do the necessary work to get there. In his case, although he would really enjoy looking like an Adonis, he will settle for something less than perfection.

Next, having established his goal, he needs to assess his present situation realistically. His naked reflection in the mirror may seem squalid and distressing; however, only by assessing his present appearance can he get the necessary information on which to base a plan of action.

Perhaps the most important element to effect change is a wish to succeed. Pious hopes and good intentions are like a rainbow: they are beautiful to see but disappear with the first change in the weather. The will to succeed must also be tempered with realism. If, for example, it usually takes several months for a man of Mr. Giant's mature years to become fit, he may be able to better the average time, but he must be realistic about the scale of the job and give it the time and effort that it needs.

As we look around the office, the local bar, or the production line, we see many people who talk about getting back in shape but cannot manage to keep fit and healthy. Ambitions are cheap; genuine commitment to change is expensive.

The following straightforward and practical activity will help you consider whether our ideas about change apply to your own experience.

Begin by writing down on a sheet of paper an action of yours that gave you some real benefit. Then think of what led up to your decision to act, and how matters progressed. Take five or ten minutes to write down these points; then ask if your list reveals the following factors:

- There was a genuine need to do something.
- You were personally committed to change.
- There was a mental picture or visualization of how things would be improved.
- Some aims were made clear.
- The task was sufficiently small to be handled successfully.
- You pursued your aim despite unexpected difficulties.

If these points apply to your experience, they are probably effective guidelines to promote future change.

Development always involves some risk and initiative; often it means going out on a limb. Therefore, it makes sense to reduce the risks by being as realistic as possible. However, management should not discourage risk taking and initiative; although doing so may promote calm, it also saps strength and energy and tends to develop obsolescent men and women who delegate responsibility to their superiors as a matter of principle. When difficulty, challenge, risk, and success do not exist, degeneration and sterility take root and thrive.

IMPROVING YOUR CHANCES OF SUCCESS

One fine day in the country, a man stopped to pass the time with a farmer who was reflectively surveying his fields. Our friend said, "There seem to be more rabbits about these days." The farmer's reply was, "Ah yes, there are more rabbits because there is less disease and we have had good weather for the grass. Last year there was a lot of fox hunting and so there were fewer predators. But they've stopped hunting the foxes this year because some of the hounds died, there are more weasels this year, and we've started shooting rabbits to eat, so next year there won't be so many rabbits."

Our friend took a deep breath and said, "Say that again, slowly." To clarify the farmer's comment, he drew a diagram to show the forces working both for and against change—respectively, driving forces and resisting forces (Lewin, 1969).

Because the forces working to decrease the rabbit population next year are stronger than the forces working to increase the rabbit population, the number of rabbits will decline.

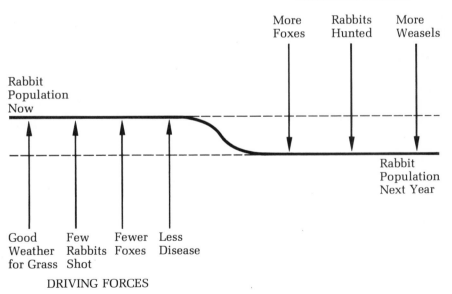

Similarly, in business situations there are forces working for change and forces working against change. The present situation is the result of the balance between these forces.

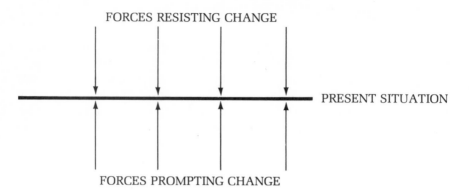

FORCES RESISTING CHANGE

PRESENT SITUATION

FORCES PROMPTING CHANGE

When we can see more clearly what these various forces mean in practice, there is a better chance of bringing about change in the direction we seek.

Once the forces on both sides are named, they can be weighed. Whereas some forces are very strong and significant, others are of little consequence. We can bring about change in two ways: either by increasing the forces prompting change or by reducing the forces resisting change. Though it is often easier and more useful to remove barriers than to crush them, nearly all successful efforts to improve situations give emphasis to both sides of the equation. By adding to the driving forces and weakening the resisting forces, there is a much better chance of achieving constructive change.

To help you consider both forces for and forces against change when planning how to deal with a difficult problem, we have devised an activity called "To Change or Not to Change" (Part Four).

SEVEN SUGGESTIONS THAT HELP CHANGE AND DEVELOPMENT

We have found that the following suggestions make sense when planning change and development.

1. Visualize clearly what the change will look like when it has been accomplished.

2. Take stock of the present situation so that you really understand what needs to be done.

3. Make a realistic plan of action that will suit your needs and be manageable in your situation.

4. Check progress and, if necessary, amend the plan in the light of your experience.

5. Help everyone discover, in his own terms, what he needs to do as part of the process.

6. Let people take risks as securely as possible and remember that sometimes innovations fail. New ventures need support, not obstruction.

7. Think about the forces that are likely to resist change and those that are likely to prompt change. Try to minimize the resisting forces and maximize the driving forces.

REFERENCE

Lewin, K. Quasi-stationary social equilibria and the problem of permanent change. In W.G. Bennis, K.D. Benne, & R. Chin (Eds.), *The planning of change* (2nd ed.). New York: Holt, Rinehart and Winston, 1969.

part two

Taking Your Organization's Temperature

Blockage Questionnaire

Thus far we have described the kinds of problems that are likely to occur in any organization. Now we want to help you begin focusing on *your* problems—the blockages that mean something to you right now. To do this, we have developed a questionnaire that consists of 110 statements about the state of affairs in your organization. We want you to look at each one of these statements and decide whether it is broadly true or false. In many cases, it may be difficult to be absolutely accurate. However, it is most important to be honest with yourself.

The more people in your organization who answer the statements, the more accurate the results of the questionnaire. Widely representative viewpoints are more likely to portray the actual situation.

Before you and your colleagues complete the questionnaire, you should decide whether to consider the questions in relation to the organization as a whole, a particular department, or a team or group. Doing so will allow you to make more valid comparisons of the results.

When you have completed the questionnaire, we will explain how to interpret the results. By that time, you will have begun to identify your key people problems.

INSTRUCTIONS FOR COMPLETING
THE BLOCKAGE QUESTIONNAIRE

1. Use the Blockage Questionnaire Answer Sheet to respond to the statements. (If other people are also going to complete the questionnaire, it is best to photocopy the answer sheet.)

2. Work through the statements, in numerical order, marking an "X" on the appropriate square of the grid if you think a statement about your organization is broadly true. If you think a statement is *not* broadly true, leave the square blank.

3. Do not spend a great deal of time considering each statement; a few seconds should be long enough.

4. Remember that the results will be worthwhile only if you are truthful.

BLOCKAGE QUESTIONNAIRE

1. The company seems to recruit as many dullards as efficient people.
2. Lines of responsibility are unclear.
3. No one seems to have a clear understanding of what causes the company's problems.
4. The organization is not short of skills, but they seem to be of the wrong kind.
5. It would help if people showed more interest in their jobs.
6. Good suggestions are not taken seriously.
7. Each department acts like a separate empire.
8. The managers believe that people come to work only for money.
9. There are no clear successors to key people.
10. People do not spend adequate time planning for the future.
11. There is much disagreement about wage rates.
12. It takes too long for people to reach an acceptable standard of performance.
13. Jobs are not clearly defined.
14. There is not enough delegation.
15. Managers do not seem to have enough time to take, training seriously.
16. There are no real incentives to improve performance, so people do not bother.
17. Unconventional ideas never get a hearing.
18. Groups do not get together and work on common problems.
19. Managers believe that tighter supervision produces increased results.
20. The organization often needs to hire new managers from the outside.
21. One of my major problems is that I do not know what is expected of me.
22. People often leave for higher wages.
23. Applicants' qualifications seem to get lower each year.
24. The organization reflects outdated standards and needs to be brought up to date.
25. Only top management participates in important decisions.

26. Departments have different attitudes on training—some take it seriously, others do not.

27. Punishments seem to be handed out more frequently than rewards.

28. The organization would be more successful if more risks were taken.

29. People are not prepared to say what they really think.

30. Managers believe that people are basically lazy.

31. The company does not try to develop people for future positions.

32. Employees are told one thing and judged on another.

33. It seems that conformity brings the best reward.

34. Too many newcomers leave quickly.

35. Different parts of the organization pull in different directions.

36. The company does not really know what talent is available.

37. Skills are picked up rather than learned systematically.

38. People are exploited—they are not rewarded adequately for the large amount of effort they exert.

39. Frequently, innovation is not rewarded.

40. In this organization it is every man for himself when the pressure is applied.

41. Managers would like to revert to the days when discipline reigned supreme.

42. Management does not identify and develop those who are potential high achievers.

43. Personal objectives have little in common with the firm's aims.

44. The payment system prevents work from being organized in the best way.

45. Many employees are only barely efficient.

46. The chief executive has so much to do that it is impossible for him to keep in touch with everything.

47. The right information needed to make decisions is not readily available.

48. The managers had to learn the hard way and think others should do the same.

49. People in the organization do not really get a thorough explanation of how their performance is valued.

50. Competing organizations seem to have brighter ideas.

51. Each manager is responsible for his own department and does not welcome interference.

52. The only reason this firm exists is to make money for the shareholders.

53. People do not know what the firm has in mind for them in the future.

54. People are judged on personal characteristics rather than on their contributions.

55. On the whole, there is no adequate method of rewarding exceptional effort.

56. There is resentment because new people seem to get the better jobs.

57. Some departments have more people than their contribution justifies.

58. The organization operates on old ideas rather than on new ones.

59. Managers are not capable of training others.

60. If the chips were down, managers would not be fully prepared to extend themselves for the firm.

61. Once something becomes an established practice it is rarely challenged.

62. Meetings are not popular because they are generally unproductive.

63. Management does not care whether people are happy in their work.

64. Management succession and development cannot be planned; there are too many variables.

65. The organization's future plans are of low quality.

66. The organization does not pay enough to attract sufficiently competent people.

67. There is really not much talent around.

68. All too often, important things either do not get done or get done twice.

69. Labor turnover figures are not calculated.

70. Production could be increased if the right skills were available.

71. I do not feel supported in what I am trying to do.

72. This is a dynamic age and the company is not moving fast enough.

73. Lessons learned in one department do not get transferred to others.

74. The firm does not try to make jobs interesting and meaningful.
75. Many people are trained who later join competitors.
76. Objectives are expressed in vague terms.
77. People have to work long hours to make an adequate living wage.
78. People with little or no talent and experience are hired.
79. Some managers are overloaded while others have it easy.
80. Employees do not know how competitive the wages are because comparative figures are not available.
81. People are not encouraged to update their skills.
82. People do not get the opportunity to contribute and, as a result, do not feel committed.
83. People do not like to "rock the boat."
84. Competition inside the organization is so fierce that it becomes destructive.
85. Managers do not think that people are interested in the quality of their working lives.
86. The experience of senior managers is not wide enough.
87. Priorities are not clear.
88. People feel as though they work in a "second-class" organization.
89. When recruiting, the firm finds it difficult to sort out the wheat from the chaff.
90. There is no use talking about reorganization; attitudes are fixed.
91. Management-control information is not generated where it is needed.
92. Quality would be improved if the staff were more skilled.
93. The firm pays below par and people are dissatisfied.
94. Managers are not sufficiently responsive to changes in the external environment.
95. People could help each other more, but they do not seem to care.
96. Managers are not addressed by their first names.
97. Managers do not believe that management education has much to offer them.
98. Plans seem unreal.
99. The firm's total "benefits package" compares unfavorably with similar organizations.
100. The organization does not have many recognized recruitment practices; individual managers do what they think best.

101. Departments do not respect the work of other groups.

102. Management does not recognize the cost of a dissatisfied employee.

103. It is not surprising that newcomers sometimes receive a poor impression of the organization, considering the way they are treated in the first few days.

104. People would welcome more challenge in their jobs.

105. Problems are not faced openly and frankly.

106. Teams do not consciously take steps to improve the way they work together.

107. There is a lot of under-the-surface fighting between managers.

108. Managers are not open about the future prospects of their people.

109. Decisions are made now that should have been made months ago.

110. I, personally, feel underpaid.

BLOCKAGE QUESTIONNAIRE ANSWER SHEET

■ Follow the instructions given at the beginning of the questionnaire.

■ In the grid below there are 110 squares, each one numbered to correspond to a question. Mark an "X" through the square if you think a statement about your organization is broadly true. If you think a statement is not broadly true, leave the square blank. Fill in the top line first, working from left to right; then fill in the second line, etc. Be careful not to miss a question.

A	B	C	D	E	F	G	H	I	J	K
1	2	3	4	5	6	7	8	9	10	11
12	13	14	15	16	17	18	19	20	21	22
23	24	25	26	27	28	29	30	31	32	33
34	35	36	37	38	39	40	41	42	43	44
45	46	47	48	49	50	51	52	53	54	55
56	57	58	59	60	61	62	63	64	65	66
67	68	69	70	71	72	73	74	75	76	77
78	79	80	81	82	83	84	85	86	87	88
89	90	91	92	93	94	95	96	97	98	99
100	101	102	103	104	105	106	107	108	109	110

Totals

■ When you have considered all 110 statements, total the number of "X's" in each vertical column and go on to the next page.

INTERPRETING THE RESULTS

In Part One we described the following eleven blockages to the effective use of people.

1. Inadequate Recruitment and Selection
2. Confused Organizational Structure
3. Inadequate Control
4. Poor Training
5. Low Motivation
6. Low Creativity
7. Poor Teamwork
8. Inappropriate Management Philosophy
9. Lack of Succession Planning and Management Development
10. Unclear Aims
11. Unfair Rewards

In the Blockage Questionnaire, you have been considering statements relating to these blockages. You can now arrive at your score for each blockage as it relates to your own organization.

Let us stress that the questionnaire has been designed only to give you an indication of where to start looking for the roots of your people problems. As such, it is not scientifically accurate, and the results will need further confirmation.

Write below the totals from each vertical column on the answer sheet.

Totals

A	
B	
C	
D	
E	
F	

Blockage 1. Inadequate Recruitment (p. 37)

Blockage 2. Confused Organizational Structure (p. 43)

Blockage 3. Inadequate Control (p. 50)

Blockage 4. Poor Training (p. 56)

Blockage 5. Low Motivation (p. 61)

Blockage 6. Low Creativity (p. 65)

G	
H	
I	
J	
K	

Blockage 7. Poor Teamwork (p. 69)

Blockage 8. Inappropriate Management Philosophy (p. 74)

Blockage 9. Lack of Succession Planning and Management Development (p. 78)

Blockage 10. Unclear Aims (p. 81)

Blockage 11. Unfair Rewards (p. 85)

The blockages with the highest scores are those that need to be explored further.

In Part Three, we take a closer look at the blockages and describe what they look like and how it feels to have them. As you read through the blockages, you should decide whether the state of affairs in your organization confirms or rejects the results of the questionnaire. Start with the two or three blockages for which you had the highest scores. As you read the details of each particular blockage, it will help to ask the following question: "Is this a real problem for us?" And, if your answer is positive, "Do we want to invest energy in solving the problem?"

At the end of each blockage essay you will be directed to relevant activities that will help you begin to explore that blockage and to work on clearing it.

part three

Eleven Common Blockages

Blockage 1 — Inadequate Recruitment and Selection

> *Experience is the name*
> *every one gives to their mistakes.*
> Oscar Wilde

We know of a small company that sells highly specialized machinery to food manufacturers. It is famous for innovation and advanced design, and recognizes that its greatest asset is the talent and creative skill of its research and development department.

Several years ago, the company needed to hire a new head of the research and development department. Because the job was so crucial to the well-being of the firm, senior managers held many conferences to determine who should be appointed. The production manager put it this way, "If we make a bad decision this time, it will be like digging a big hole and jumping in."

Because it is common fantasy to believe that outside people are somehow more capable and resourceful than those already in the organization, the management decided that none of the scientists working in the department possessed the necessary qualities to become manager. So the vacant post was advertised. The directors had lunch with the final list of applicants, and one man impressed everyone as being outstanding. He was a management consultant whose style was to ask basic and challenging questions. The directors were certain that his approach to business would be immensely valuable.

Without involving the department in the selection process, the management consultant was hired. Whispers of concern preceded him, and further investigations indicated some problems in his background. Nevertheless, the company prepared to welcome him.

It took nearly a year for the scale of the disaster to sink in. The ex-consultant was good at asking questions, but not at answering them. His colleagues and subordinates were driven wild by the pattern of provoking questions, delayed decisions, and frightened withdrawal in the face of attack. His behavior antagonized them to such an extent that confusion and frustration intensified within the development team.

Channels of decision making became choked with weed and blocked by the rotting hulks of unresolved issues. The senior scientist, a man whose main interests lay in obscure calculations, eventually found it necessary to write the following memorandum on January 7th: "Could I please have a reply to my memo of December 6, which asked for a reply to my memo of October 11?"

The development manager responded to the attacks by withdrawing into increasingly detailed but meaningless work and finally left with a nervous breakdown. It took another six months to collect the pieces and to build the department again; a total of two years had been virtually wasted. Eventually, the company decided to write down the lessons, which sound like the warnings given to Julius Caesar on the Ides of March, to help avoid making the same mistakes again.

- Beware of a silver tongue and check for real achievement.
- Let the team choose its own leaders as much as possible.
- Be careful about managers who appear distant, confusing, or arrogant.
- Never underestimate the time and care needed to choose people wisely.

A poor recruitment and selection decision often leads to a whole series of serious problems for years to come. Recruiting someone who lacks the capacity to do a job to the required standard means that the job is badly done, that standards as a whole deteriorate, that colleagues get frustrated, and that the person concerned usually becomes a permanent fixture because it is difficult for him or her to get another job. In addition, to rub salt into the wound, the person often feels undervalued, and spends countless hours grumbling and complaining that no one understands him.

Time-study engineers have clicked their stop watches often enough to know that the best employee at any level will be many times more useful than the worst; therefore, it is important to hire people who can "deliver the goods."

This discrepancy between the performance of the best and the worst is a serious problem in skilled and repetitive jobs, but it can be a first-order disaster at the management level. An incompetent manager distresses his staff, bungles many tasks he undertakes, and, tragically, runs lethargically away from opportunities. He not only makes a substandard contribution himself, but he inhibits his subordinates and colleagues to such an extent that the total negative effect he creates is far greater than anyone would dare calculate.

People can and do develop, but they rarely undergo a personal revolution. It is naive to expect a major change in the character of mature people. Few believe that a Twiggy can be "developed" into a Raquel Welch, or a street-corner fiddler into a Yehudi Menuhin, but many managers believe they can bring about change on a similar scale in their subordinates.

While some features of personality and skill can be changed by training and experience, it is always an arduous process, and any real development in personality is largely dependent on the perception and willingness of the individual concerned. If a person lacks basic intelligence, judgment, or sensitivity to other people, experience teaches us that substantial change is unlikely. After all, there is not much point in exerting major effort trying to make square pegs fit round holes if round pegs can be acquired in the first place.

In a firm that has poor recruitment and selection practices, managers often complain that applicants' qualifications get lower and lower each year and that people take too long to reach an acceptable standard of work. Yet there are as many intelligent, able, and adaptable people in the population as ever. If your own organization does not have the quality of people it needs, this is a warning signal telling you that your recruitment approach needs care and control.

Managers may blame their lack of talent on the changing attitudes of people and society at large, but often it boils down to the fact that the organization's own attitudes and methods have remained fixed in the past, thereby producing an environment or style that overlooks people's needs and concerns.

All sorts of things make up the atmosphere in a firm; restrooms, desks, notices, colors, heating, hours of work, supervisors, status of work, and hundreds of other large and small matters combine to produce a particular style. But styles, like clothes, tend to go out of fashion. People choose whom they wish to work for and can usually choose to go elsewhere. Consequently, it pays to keep in touch with their needs and with the environment at large.

A good index of your company's real attitude toward people is to see how many newcomers leave after a few weeks. Many firms irritate, bore, and subtly humiliate people from their first moments as employees. Managers then blame their high staff turnover on the fickle, irresponsible attitudes of people today. They need to realize that, as it says in *Julius Caesar*, "The fault, dear Brutus, is not in our stars, but in ourselves, that we are underlings."

An organization's stock of talent is another crucial issue. To be capable of sustaining health and seizing new opportunities, a firm needs to have a stock of available talent. The firm that has large numbers of people who are only "just good enough" for their present jobs finds real difficulty in achieving more and in growing bigger. People, particularly managers and supervisors, need to be capable of growing and developing with the organization. The lesson is obvious: recruitment and selection should have an eye on the future as well as on immediate needs.

But there is a point to be careful of here. Take care *not* to under-utilize people. They will become frustrated and angry and then seek a new employer.

COMMON RECRUITING FAULTS

Many errors can be made when recruiting people. A frequent blunder occurs because managers seldom keep statistical records of the rate at which people move in and out of the organization. Every firm we know that has taken the trouble to calculate its labor turnover rates and lengths of service has found opportunities to save on the cost of recruitment. Studies show that the cost of hiring one person is more than equivalent to his first month's salary. If a manager overspent the same amount on carbon paper, people would laugh about it for years, but no one gives more than a shrug when a recruit leaves before he has contributed anything.

A second error in recruiting is not defining what kind of man or woman you want to hire. Generally, a person is recruited with a particular job in mind. But if no one develops a list of qualities and qualifications that the successful applicant will need, then some important points are bound to be missed at the interview stage.

Third, interviews are often superficial and unorganized. Sometimes, because of inexperience or incompetence, an interviewer is more nervous than the candidate himself and, to hide this, spends more time talking than the applicant.

Generations of managers have been encouraged to use some simple, systematic approach to recruitment and selection, yet we constantly see evidence that even the most rudimentary points are overlooked. One manager we know used to start his interviews by asking, "Have you a criminal record?" After that, a free exchange of views was hard to achieve!

A fourth recruiting fault occurs when there is an unwillingness to use outside help or aids in the selection process. If you want to measure a young man's potential as an apprentice engineer, conversations alone are likely to be inferior to structured interviews combined with a good set of tests designed for that purpose. When recruiting for an important job or where large numbers of people with similar skills are recruited, a fairly small expenditure on aids and external advice can repay its initial cost time and time again. Even if an individual stays with you for only a few years, he is going to represent a fair-sized investment.

Many companies try to solve their recruitment problems by enlarging their personnel department. Unfortunately, although fine in principle, many personnel departments are the homes of failed executives who are out of touch with the needs of line managers and who spend their time doing things that those managers could do better themselves. A good personnel department can add tremendous depth to management practice; however, an incompetent personnel function is worse than useless because it takes over important tasks and bungles them. The people who really care about recruitment are those who have to work directly with the new employees.

RECRUITING AND SELECTION PROCEDURES

Because selection and recruitment are difficult, costly, competitive, and very important, many companies have adopted more systematic procedures to prevent past mistakes. As you read the steps we describe below, compare them with your own firm's approach. You can then formulate a working discipline from your own personal experiences and observations.

- Make a list of the tasks you expect the person to perform and describe the overall contribution expected. Check with those who are closely involved to see whether your expectations are accurate.
- List the experience and personal qualities that are necessary to do the job well.
- Consider the likely future of this person in five years and the implications of this for selection.
- When setting the salary, remember that those who pay peanuts get monkeys.
- Place realistic advertisements in the most relevant publications.
- See that the interviews are properly planned and are conducted by more than one person.
- Consider the physical side of the interviews; for instance, candidates are more likely to talk freely if both interviewer and applicant are seated at the same table or if they face each other in comfortable chairs.
- Encourage the applicant to ask questions and be frank in your replies, giving a completely realistic picture of the available job.

- Get advice and help on really important choices from experienced advisers, but do not rely on their judgment excessively. You have to work with the person selected; the expert does not.
- Remember that selection is a two-way process. Really useful people are invariably in short supply, and they can pick employers who offer the best rewards.
- The recruitment process is not complete when the man or woman has accepted your offer. His first few weeks at work, in particular, are crucial, and there should be careful effort to involve him in his job and with the organization.

In the ideal situation, all positions within the company are filled by people with the necessary intelligence, ability, experience, education, and personal qualities to do their jobs really well. In addition, sufficient potential should be developed to meet the possible future needs of the business. This is a pretty tall order and will never be entirely achieved, but we can hope for a situation where most opportunities are profitably seized.

Recruitment is often an irregular and unpredictable task, with the element of intuition playing a part in the end. But with care, recruitment disasters can be avoided. The effect of recruiting a really good person is often much greater than expected. Good people are real resources—true sources of strength—for any organization.

Suggested Activities for Blockage 1—Inadequate Recruitment and Selection

Blockage 2 — Confused Organizational Structure

Insight without action breeds anxiety.
Action without insight breeds confusion.
Inspired by Barry A. Goodfield

No matter how businesses are organized, people will probably complain that the total effect is frustrating, impersonal, and often inefficient. Yet, despite all the difficulties, organizations are necessary features of our society. They are our friends, and we need to know their strengths and weaknesses and to learn how to make them serve us.

Whenever people are grouped together there are the inevitable problems of coordinating effort. Those in smaller units have a much greater chance of winning the fight against organizational sloth and sterility. As firms grow in size, however, the question of organization becomes a more involved and important issue, one that demands careful thought; otherwise, the difficulties of getting things done become so great that people are liable to give up trying and just concentrate on keeping their noses clean.

The simplest type of business is a one-man band. Consider, for example, a dealer in firewood. Every morning he collects wood, carries it to his house, chops it, and travels through town knocking on doors and selling it. Suppose business booms and he decides to take on some extra help. He then must decide who chops, who collects the wood, who sells it, and how the different activities relate. In the early days, there will be few headaches over organization, but, as the business expands, the woodcutter will have to learn how to delegate, a function many managers find difficult, especially in smaller businesses. As a small business grows, so does the need to have a recognizable structure and a clear definition of who does what.

Learning how to organize is one of the problems that nag top management the most. Who does what or who controls what is probably the biggest cause of rows, recriminations, and undercover fighting. A person building a business often has so many nasty experiences that he believes the only one he can trust is himself and that other people are either too limited or unreliable or are out to take him for a ride at the first opportunity.

Some managers have very fixed ideas about how every human situation should be organized, but every organization has to adapt and grow with the situation of the moment.

AUTHORITY AND CONTROL

The organization of a firm is the result of thousands of decisions made by the people who work there. Yet once precedents become established and the attitudes of influential people become enshrined as the company's spirit or "culture," people rarely take a step back and ask whether the firm's basic beliefs and assumptions are still valid or morally right.

One of the trends over the past twenty years has been an increasing tendency to define and to limit the contribution of each worker. This may seem logical to management, but we often see it linked to poor performance, low job satisfaction, and industrial disputes.

A small group of managers in Topeka, Kansas, organized a new pet food plant based on innovative principles, which were designed to reduce management controls and to organize the workers into self-managing teams (Walton, 1972). The work was planned to be as interesting and meaningful as possible. The teams were responsible for recruiting, upgrading, scheduling, training, and even contributing to budgeting and planning. The aim was to involve people in the decisions that affected them and to make each job a learning experience. Visiting this factory today is a thought-provoking experience. The employees have real enthusiasm for their jobs and feel responsible for the success of their plant. It comes as no surprise to learn that output figures are consistently and substantially better than comparable plants.

The essential difference at the Topeka plant is that important issues are dealt with by everyone, rather than by a small group of the elite. It does not have a small, insular group of managers who sit in deep-pile-carpeted offices making decisions about people as if they were machines.

That people differ widely in their attitudes toward authority is an important aspect. Perhaps the most common difference is between those who wish to keep authority and control with the boss (autocratic style) and those who want to distribute authority and control more widely (participative style). Although both methods have worked well in some situations and have failed in others, it is most important to achieve an organizational and managerial style that fits the needs of the situation at a particular time. Today, many industrialists feel that they are experiencing a major need to shift away from autocracy towards more participative management approaches.

Autocratic Style

In the autocratic approach, which centralizes control, decisions can be made quickly and uniformity is insured. Employees, however, have little or no influence in decision making. This system of management has many levels, clear job demarcations, and defined procedures. Unfortunately, everyone but the boss feels like a puppet. The boss holds the strings, writes the lines, and directs the play. Others do not get a chance to influence events. Some people, who dislike responsibilities, enjoy this, but many get angry and depressed under an authoritarian regime. This is especially true when the man or woman at the center is incompetent or inhumane. It is one thing to be led by a person who has the qualities of wisdom, humanity, and purpose; it is quite another to be ruled by a person who has the qualities of stupidity and bungling ineptitude.

In a situation where there is a very strong, autocratic boss, often subordinates do not get a chance to develop, and, as a result, they often acquire the servile mentality of a school boy in a Dickens novel.

Participative Style

The participative approach is a more difficult management philosophy to practice, yet it has been associated with many high-performing managers throughout the world. Perhaps the most common characteristics are that each person is involved in matters that affect him and that the organization cares about individuals' needs. Clear procedures and demarcations may develop, but they are formed from within rather than imposed from above.

On the positive side, the participative style of management can lead to increased motivation and communication, while encouraging a team approach to common tasks. On the other hand, it can create more problems because a wider distribution of views is taken into account, which may result in excuses for inaction, vacillation, and confusion.

It has been said that the best place to make decisions is where the problem hurts. However, unless there is an organization-wide perspective on team building, work groups may satisfy their own needs rather than those of the organization.

EFFECTS OF ENVIRONMENT AND TECHNOLOGY

Another important consideration in a firm's organization is the influence of environment and technology. Basically, companies need to be organized according to the requirements of their particular technology.

And each particular technology requires specific abilities from people. Therefore, a company concerned with rapid technological innovation is organized differently from one making handmade replicas of Chippendale chairs.

To illustrate, we will take a look at four different types of firms and the principles that guide them.

Firms on the Frontiers of Knowledge

These firms are the innovators, often working on the application of science to the world at large. Nothing is certain except that change will be an everyday event.

With these firms, an open structure of free-flowing, autonomous groups is usually most effective. Colleagues work closely together because they are venturing into the unknown, and a great respect for individual professionalism and creativity is fostered. The role of management in such an environment principally involves channelling resources and defining uncertain situations in terms that can be understood. Moves towards bureaucracy are usually symptomatic of middle age, where rigid systems replace genuine, creative thought.

Firms Dealing with Craft Jobs

Many firms make specialized products with a known and stable technology. There is no attempt to go into uncharted waters, although a wide range of problems must be tackled. The craftsman, who applies the skill and experience of half a lifetime, is the pivot, backed by squads of service people. In this situation, management tends to be more systematic and hierarchical, with clear lines of decision making. To a great extent, important details are left to the man doing the job.

Firms in Process Production

When a range of products is produced continuously, usually the production pattern can be carefully planned; often it remains virtually unchanged for years. Although individual jobs are often routine and repetitive, the cost of inadequate performance can be high. Management decisions tend to be made at the senior levels, with little authority below top management. Often, a weighty procedures manual is the manager's bible, and carefully arranged status charts are adhered to with a religious fervor. Management in this situation is predictable and planned, until there is a crisis or a major upheaval.

Firms with Many Customers

When a firm has many customers, especially if they come personally to use the service, e.g., a department store, it is usually a hybrid organization that has a character of its own. Managers must keep an ear to the marketplace and remain in close touch with customer needs. Creativity, often apparent at quite low levels, creates freshness and flair. Staff members often come and go with the seasons, or even more frequently.

Appropriate Organization Structure

In the 1930s, writers of management produced dozens of books advising managers how to organize. Their concepts read like a search for the pot of gold at the end of the rainbow. The pundits believed a secret principle existed that, once discovered, would yield an orderly, invincible, and profitable formula for building a perfect business machine. Unfortunately, the search was misguided and the single ideal organization proved a myth. Through research, however, more systematic ways have been found to get a good "fit" between the management structure and the technology of a firm. Some ideas are suggested in the activity "Technology and Structure" (see Part Four).

The desired situation in an organization is for the division of labor to be the best possible compromise between the jobs that have to be done (technology) and the desire of people who work there to have satisfying and meaningful jobs. There should also be sufficient flexibility within the structure to adapt to changing situations, and a way of helping people develop for their future. A good organization structure is like a fit body: each function contributes individually and the whole is well coordinated.

Symptoms of Bad Organization

A bad structure is a very costly ailment that can result in the organization firing on four cylinders out of six. Functions that are unimportant or even irrelevant can grow all out of proportion when a powerful, self-seeking manager creates a vast empire that is nothing more than a monument to himself. The appearance of such an organization resembles a beer drinker whose body is in poor shape but whose right arm is well muscled from lifting endless glasses of beer.

Issues often are left unresolved. Most companies have at least one dullard who has been shoved into a nitch where, hopefully, not too much damage will result. Often he has had a managerial job, but because he no longer has the perseverance, energy, or imagination to do that job successfully and because the organization thinks it owes him some kind of debt, he is put out to grass, perhaps in the personnel department. There he sits bungling or blocking every useful idea that comes his way. A first test of a company that wants to improve its organization is to face issues like this in a strong and humane way.

Another familiar symptom of bad organization is that some jobs are not accomplished at all. We know of one company that put a lot of energy into efficiently transporting materials two hundred miles for processing. Because no one was responsible for considering whether it would be cheaper to close the distant plant and to build an extension to the home factory, this situation lasted for eight years before anyone was made aware of the wasted energy involved.

There are widespread views on the merits of job descriptions ranging from "a necessity for any job" to "a strait-jacket that stifles initiative." Again, it is necessary to ask where you stand and whether any job-definition problems, such as the following, affect your firm: Does management have difficulty deciding on real priorities? Does management waste time doing unnecessary things? Do you have doubts about the necessity of some jobs? Is achievement sometimes measured unrealistically? Are there "who-does-what" disputes?

Organization is a very subtle and confusing subject, one that needs to be watched carefully. A structure that is completely appropriate and alive today may become unsatisfactory and dead in a few months or years. But there are no magic formulas, and another company's organization can never be completely appropriate to your own situation. Therefore, the objective is to form a structure that suits your own particular circumstances, which may involve difficult choices between opposites every step of the way.

The organization of a firm is a living network of communication, discussion, consultation, and decision making. When it works well, an infinitely larger quantity of human potential is put to constructive use. Organization is about people's lives.

REFERENCE

Walton, R. E. How to counter alienation in the plant. *Harvard Business Review*, Nov.-Dec., 1972, pp. 70-82.

**Suggested Activities for Blockage 2—Confused
Organizational Structure**

Blockage 3 — Inadequate Control

> *I think one must finally*
> *take one's life in one's arms.*
> Arthur Miller

We have two friends with very similar business problems. One built up a very successful manufacturing company. He owned a Mercedes, a motor cruiser, and two color television sets, but he did not really enjoy them because he was a worried man. You could almost see his hairs turning gray, one by one, as you talked to him. As he put it, "Things are going wrong in my business and I don't know where to kick." Although parts of his company were doing well, others were spoiling the picture, and he did not know which functions were causing the problems.

Our second friend was sitting in his office one morning feeling very cheerful because his balance sheet for the previous financial year showed a fantastic profit. Now you might assume that he had nothing to be concerned about, but the profit worried him because it came as a complete surprise, and it would have been no more surprising if the profit had been a loss.

Both of our friends had control problems. They ran successful companies but they were not really in control of what was happening.

Control problems usually start to plague a business when it is expanding. In the early stages of a firm's development, the owner is intimately concerned with all aspects of everyday business life. As the firm grows, though, he must accept the fact that he can no longer make all the decisions. Many owners of businesses, who have real difficulty accepting this, cling to the traditional tasks they have always performed. We even know of one highly successful senior manager who still insists on personally opening and locking his factory door each day. The consequences of such managerial gluttony can easily lead to incompetence or a nervous breakdown.

At the other extreme is the man who delegates everything, even the really crucial things, without maintaining any form of control over what has been delegated.

As a business expands, it becomes imperative to develop systems of control that will largely look after themselves. Many businesses have floundered into confusion, gloom, hysteria, and eventually bankruptcy because they lacked basic control procedures.

Effective Control

In our experience, effective control has the following characteristics:

- Relevant information is gathered quickly and is presented in a clear, concise manner.
- Opportunities for open discussion help problems to be clearly identified and worked through.
- Decisions are made on a rational basis, with proper planning of resources.
- Policies are reviewed to improve future performance.
- People at all levels are involved in measuring their own performance.

Lack of Control

Although control is a complex subject, the symptoms are often quite obvious. An example is the manager who is unable to cope with all the demands on his time and who performs like a player in a speeded-up silent movie.

We know of one factory manager who had so many problems controlling his production that he never really functioned as an executive. You would often hear something like this in his factory:

> "Joe, Unifoods has been on the phone again asking where its order is. You know we promised it by the 20th, so where the hell is it?"
>
> "I'm sorry, Pete, but the stores were out of widgets again and by the time we got them, the assembly department was busy on that order for Smith."
>
> "Well, you're in charge of assembly, it's your job to sort it out. Why do you let this happen? You should arrange it ahead of time with the stores."
>
> "I don't run stores, you know, and sales shouldn't promise things without consulting us. Anyway, you are in charge, so it is your job to make sure everything is coordinated properly."
>
> "I haven't got ten pairs of hands, you know. I spend all my time sorting out shop floor problems now."

Obviously, the production manager had a control problem, and he was at the center of it. Even though everyone in the department knew problems existed, no one knew how to examine them carefully enough to prevent their reoccurring.

The remedy needed in this case was not an elaborate production-control system. All that was needed was a simple system that signalled a red light when a problem needed attention—in this case, short and regular production meetings, during which any problems and issues were dealt with openly and targets and plans were laid for the following week.

Although the first few meetings were rather sordid, characterized by managers voicing old grievances, once all the "dirt" was brought out into the open, reasons for shortcomings started to be discussed freely, and everyone began to find the meetings valuable. The senior man was better able to control what happened in the factory, and managers, instead of feeling tied down by targets and plans, saw the meetings as sources of help. The manager, instead of spending most of his time racing around the factory fire-fighting, was able to spend more of his time thinking and acting on the really important things that he used to neglect. As a result of the regular meetings, the reasons for variance from plans were examined and problems diminished in frequency.

Control Belongs to Management

One of the key skills of professional management is to develop ways to bring order to complicated situations. Although many consultancies are solely concerned with developing such effective control systems, we need to be wary of letting consultants solve our problems for us. Control is an inalienable management function; it cannot be subcontracted to an outside expert. However many instant solutions they read in books or hear in courses, managers must learn for themselves how to achieve and maintain control over their areas of responsibility, how to make up their own minds concerning what is "too much" control and what is "too little" control. Those who do not face these issues themselves become weaker and ineffective. (See also the Appendix, Outside Help—Advantages and Snags.)

A manager needs to have a clear notion of normal and acceptable standards and to have fast ways to determine exactly what is going wrong.

Various activities in a business require different forms of control. In the financial arena, control is generally associated with establishing cost and stock control systems, knowing which products create profits and losses, and having adequate stocks at the lowest cost. But effective control is more than just forms and bookkeeping systems, which never portray the entire picture. The people who operate those systems are equally important.

The way a firm develops is determined largely by the kinds of decisions managers make. Controlling a firm as a whole is largely a question of knowing when and where the important decisions are being made and how they affect the firm. It is impossible to do this successfully just with forms and bookkeeping systems, since it is much more a question of how managers communicate, of what they talk to the boss about, and of the quality of relationships involved.

People Are Not Machines

The control of machine performance is an engineering question, but with people, control is very much an emotional issue. Probably all of us, as children, experienced discipline and reacted against it at one time or another. If people are tied down by a control system that makes them feel stifled, at worst they will give up trying, and at best they will find some way of manipulating the system to their advantage. On the other hand, if they are treated responsibly and feel accountable for their own actions, then they will see control as supportive and necessary.

This relates to the form of leadership managers take—a democratic (or participative) approach, or an autocratic (or authoritarian) approach. (See also Blockage 2.) A manager, through his leadership style, has the power to create a nurturing, creative climate for his employees, or one that leads to sterility, conformity, hostility, and rebellion.

A major problem with control is how perceptions and values appear in a different perspective when viewed from the management level and from the employee level. For example, something that appears to be entirely logical to the boss or to another department may be interpreted as unjust and ridiculous to the people lower in the organizational hierarchy who are affected by the decisions. Take one organization we know very well. It was once a small outfit where managers of the operating divisions controlled their own people without much interference from the head office. Because people worked largely on their own, the managers realized that any form of control needed to be supportive and not inhibitive. As one manager put it, "If a guy is on his own for 90 percent of his working life, then he really has to be responsible for his own actions."

But soon the company expanded; three operating divisions turned into seven, and circumstances changed. Someone at the head office decided that more control was needed. Unfortunately, instead of working through the division managers, the head office tried to assume control by designing forms, instituting systems, and issuing instructions. Soon thereafter, control began to be seen as inhibitive rather than supportive, and the staff began to wonder whether they were reporting to their own manager or some bureaucrat at the head office. The people at the head office did not understand the real problems of operating the divisions, and their lack of knowledge showed in the paper work they designed. The managers of the operating divisions, incensed by the usurping of their own positions, felt that they were in conflict with the head office and resorted to designing their own systems. Within six months, trade-union membership in the operating divisions rose from 8 to 75 percent, just one measure of how the workers felt about the situation. The people at the head office could not understand the resentment; as far as they were concerned, they were simply doing what was necessary and trying to be helpful.

Another friend of ours, who had all the trappings of a successful businessman, also illustrates how perceptions and values can change according to status and position. Usually he drove his luxurious sports car with an executive dash, but one day he needed to drive a five-ton truck. Much to his amazement, his whole attitude changed as he sat behind the driving wheel—he carved up private cars, showed friendly courtesy to other commercial-vehicle drivers, and leered at passing girls. He was surprised that a change in his apparent position in society should have such an immediate effect on his behavior.

Managerial Skill

Many really successful managers feel that their key skill lies in knowing when to stand back, when to get involved, when to consult, when to make decisions, and, perhaps most difficult of all, when to say "yes" and when to say "no."

If a manager can detect potential trouble spots and keep control supportive, he will be able to spend more time on key management functions. He will also avoid becoming chronically overloaded with unimportant details and gradually sinking into a morass of confusion while others watch with cynical amusement or irritation.

Suggested Activities for Blockage 3—Inadequate Control

Blockage 4 — Poor Training

All living organisms adapt,
or they cease to exist.
Louis E. Davis

A colleague and friend of ours has spent a lot of time visiting firms in the meat industry, offering advice on how to teach manual skills in a better way. He often tells the story of a master butcher who demonstrated how he taught knife sharpening.

Although the butcher was obviously very skilled, it was noticeable that he had quite a collection of scars on his hand where the knife had slipped. When asked how he accounted for them, the butcher replied, "Well, you have to learn in any job, don't you? Getting cut is part of it."

The master butcher found it hard to imagine that there were better ways of learning than the trial-and-error methods of his apprenticeship. Fortunately, he decided to try some of the "systematic" training techniques advocated by specialists. Much to his surprise, he found that careful instruction reduced learning time and accidents and that there was no need to acquire a patchwork of scars when learning to use a knife.

A great deal of learning takes place each day in organizations. People acquire new skills, gain insights into new ideas and knowledge, and learn how to achieve better results. In many cases, formal approaches to learning can often be more helpful than the traditional trial-and-error methods.

This is particularly true when a new person joins an organization. Inevitably, he lacks some kind of knowledge and skill and needs to know what company procedures are, what is required of him, and even where to hang his coat. Since he may need to learn how to operate a machine or how to keep a set of books, a choice has to be made—will he learn by a thoughtfully constructed induction program, or will he pick up a skill from "Willie," the old hand?

New knowledge and skills are often difficult to acquire. Therefore, whenever a job takes a fair amount of time to learn or when specific skills need to be acquired, it is worthwhile to develop a systematic approach to help the new person reach a satisfactory standard with a minimum of time, cost, and stress. Similarly, it is necessary to provide the right opportunities for some people to be promoted to higher-level jobs, so they will become the supervisors and managers that the organization needs in the future. When these training opportunities are not available, people may not learn and develop in ways beneficial to both the firm and the individual.

Costs of Poor Training

Although we often measure the cost of machine maintenance and depreciation down to the second decimal place, training is sometimes viewed as an unfortunate operating cost rather than as an investment for the future. It is relatively easy to buy a new machine or even to build a new factory, but it is often more difficult to obtain the creative element of a business—the people who make an organization thrive or fail.

We have seen many cases where the lack of suitably trained people has cost the company dearly in needless time and expense. The following situations are frequent.

Situation	Result
A company functions below capacity because no one can operate the equipment.	Under-used plant
Employees function below par.	Low production
New employees need to keep asking "Willie" questions.	Interruption to other workers
People get frustrated because they are not helped to settle down; often they leave before they are fully skilled, thus putting the organization to the cost of recruiting and training again.	Low morale
Employees cannot operate the plant and the machinery efficiently or inspect products properly.	Increased wastage and low quality

If a few calculations of these costs were made, perhaps training would be taken more seriously and would receive higher priority.

Recruiting and training involve more than costs; they also involve attitudes. Whenever a person joins your organization, he or she gets an instant impression of whether you care about employees. Lip service and fancy statements in the employee handbook or on the bulletin board are not as impressive as the actual experience of the first few working days.

Perhaps a new employee did not know where to report, was left hanging around for hours, or found people unhelpful and uninterested. Managers and staff who treat a new recruit with indifference or neglect often color that person's impression of the firm for months.

MANAGEMENT TRAINING AND COMPETENCE

Every individual must take personal responsibility for his own learning and development—this is the essence of personal growth. It is unfortunate that many training systems and methods try to manipulate people rather than to help them develop their own resources more effectively. In reality, an organization can only create the opportunity and climate for learning to occur; the individual himself is responsible for his own personal growth. Therefore, it is important for a trainee to clarify his own views about his needs and to accept responsibility for what happens.

At the management level, learning is almost the cornerstone of success. Today, in such rapidly changing times, there is no room for fixed attitudes and yesterday's approaches. In a hurricane, the trees that bend and move end up standing, while those that are rigid and unyielding are left broken and uprooted.

Theories on the nature of management competence abound with lists describing the qualities, traits, and abilities of successful managers. The four key abilities that these lists often contain are (1) control, (2) innovation, (3) harnessing people's energies and putting them to use, and (4) integration with the organization as a whole. If control is lacking, there is confusion; if there is no innovation, rigor mortis quickly sets in; if people's energies are not harnessed, the result is often sloth and rebellion; and if integration is not present, there is empire building.

However, even though these ideas contain a basis of truth, a man or a woman can have all the necessary qualities and still not be a good manager. Something else is needed to make the difference between success and failure.

Management competence involves not only having the necessary knowledge and skill, but also having the vital capacity to seize opportunities, to stimulate action, to venture ahead, to make decisions, to stand up and be counted, and to take a measure of risk. Without such action, management just does not exist; it is only theory. No textbook or paper qualification can give a person that capacity; in the end, it involves learning by experience, exposing oneself to difficulty and risk, and learning from successes and mistakes. The organization can aid the learning process by providing the opportunity and a measure of support; but when the chips are down, the manager is responsible for his own development.

Systematic Training

Organizing the learning process is more difficult than it appears at first sight. Often the most difficult aspect is recognizing that something needs to be done and identifying what it is. To help bring some clarity, many companies have organized their training on a "systematic" footing.

There are various "brands" of systematic training, but the cornerstones usually involve:

(1) an assessment of the overall training needs based on the future plans and current problems of the organization;
(2) an allocation of corporate responsibility for training and for the detailed mechanics of implementing it;
(3) the preparation of training plans on an individual or group basis;
(4) training conducted by trained instructors according to the plan;
(5) keeping some form of training record;
(6) a review of the results and costs of the effort.

Shortcomings of Systematic Training

Systematic training is fine in many situations and has brought many benefits to organizations, but there are also dangers to avoid. First, training can become a religion, with everyone preaching its virtues and no one questioning them. Small firms, particularly, often are not systematic in most of the things they do. This can result in their being more dynamic and creative. Having highly systematic training when other business functions are not systematic is like having a standard-sized human body with one arm five feet long—it is out of proportion with everything else.

A second training snag concerns the false sense of security that systems often bring: "Sure we do this or that—we have a system for it." But every so often the system does not bring results, not because it is a bad system, but because other, more important matters—like the commitment of managers to the system, or the quality of relationships between people—are neglected. The system can easily take control if you stop questioning the relevance of what you originally intended it to accomplish.

As Ron Johnson, a friend of ours, says, "Training is no longer a question of injecting people with doses of skill and knowledge. It is the management of learning, helping people cope with changes in their working lives."

Suggested Activities for Blockage 4—Poor Training

Blockage 5 — Low Motivation

If men define situations as real,
they are real in their consequences.
Robert K. Merton

Successful army generals, football team managers, school teachers, and political leaders have all found the crucial importance of people's commitment to the task at hand.

The ability to do a particular job is one thing, but wanting to do it is quite another. History is full of situations where people have succeeded in achieving a particular goal, despite almost impossible odds.

Although different kinds of leadership are relevant to accomplishing various tasks, especially important is the ability to find the right keys to unlock the latent energy in people and to harness it to the task at hand. This is a rare skill, one that depends on a leader's wisdom and emotions; but when this skill is used well and when people really feel the importance of a particular action, they will make considerable efforts to achieve results.

Unfortunately, industry rarely considers in depth the way people feel about management or about the organization of their work. Rebellion, resistance, malice, and lack of interest are common in organizations throughout the world.

Two or three generations ago it was accepted, without question, that work was a necessary part of life. Students at universities diligently attended classes in suits and ties and groomed themselves for a career in industry. Today, much has changed, and many more options are available. Doubts about the overriding value of materialism and security have riddled the younger generation, and the accepted principles of our fathers are increasingly questioned. Fortunately, many organizations have adapted to the expectations of the new generation, but not without conflict and stress. Managers, in particular, tend to move in circles that support their own thinking; yet, however difficult, it is essential for them to discover what motivates and influences people.

A Person's Self-Worth

If an employee feels alienated from his place of work, then he has not entered into a meaningful "contract," and he will invest only the minimum energy to perform an assigned task.

One of the basic characteristics of man is his evaluation of his self-worth. Many of us lack a strong belief in our own value and need to have our significance confirmed. The amount of time we spend at the office and the social importance of our occupations make it inevitable that the way we are valued at work affects our attitudes toward ourselves, our community, and our employer.

One method of determining our worth to our employers is by the amount of cash we receive at the end of the week. Many managers feel that this is by far the most important factor and that everything else is irrelevant or "soft soap." But cash is *not* everything; there are other ways of showing an individual's worth.

Consider the person on welfare. Even though he may receive adequate cash, without meaningful work he begins to lose his sense of self-value; and loss of esteem, more than anything else, prevents man from achieving his inherent capabilities.

Many may not agree, but evidence confirms that work itself is much more important to most people than the cash in their weekly paycheck, provided that they are not consumed by passionate grievances about being underpaid. As the influence of money as a driving force declines, the psychological contract becomes more significant. (However, see also Blockage 11—Unfair Rewards.)

In a way, we are all investing about 30 percent of our lifetime at work. Another 30 percent is spent sleeping. If you add to this the 10 percent when we are either too young to realize or too old to cope, it becomes clear that there is relatively little time left over. In addition, work not only occupies a large proportion of our lifetime, it also occupies those hours when we are at our brightest. The stake we all have in our working lives is immense, and many feel that it is one of the tragedies of our times that so many people have lost the feeling that their work is, in any way, meaningful.

According to Frederick Herzberg (1973), an American psychologist who has worked extensively on problems of motivation, if you ask people what satisfied them most in their working lifetime, more often than not they will tell you about some tricky aspect of their job that they managed to do well. In other words, their satisfaction came from achievement rather than from payment, clean lavatories, or a company outing, the things that managers usually provide to satisfy the needs of employees.

There are two important lessons to be learned from Herzberg's research.

- We often assume that we know what other people's needs are, but we are frequently wrong.
- The financial and welfare practices that a company follows are important, but they do not, by themselves, motivate people to improve.

High vs. Low Motivation

It is commonly observed that a highly motivated person puts care and energy into the fire of his enthusiasm. Where the opposite is the case, especially if the situation is enforced, a dull, negative, and even destructive reaction is often present.

Nowhere is high motivation more apparent than with a newly married husband. He will rush home early, take flowers to his wife, and give up drinking with the boys. We would say, to use the current jargon, "He's highly motivated to please his new bride."

On the other hand, the older man who uses every excuse to keep away from his wife exhibits low motivation. In all likelihood, he will seek other ways of satisfying his needs, like drinking or even keeping pigeons.

If we have a need and we satisfy it, then it ceases to be a need. Take air, for example. Usually we do not feel a need for air because it exists plentifully everywhere. But if we are caught underwater and are unable to breathe, then the desire for air becomes the most important need in our existence. The same is generally true for food and drink, warmth, sex, and all other physiological needs (Maslow, 1970).

When basic physical needs are fulfilled, people generally seek their social needs—security, affection, family, and social position. After this stage, man seeks higher aims—the recognition and activation of his own potential and the search to find deeper meaning in life.

Human drive and energy result when individuals strive to satisfy their needs. If a company provides an environment fostering satisfaction, it will enable people to meet their needs.

A company that frustrates people is usually characterized by low motivation. Visitors can sense the lack of life and atmosphere as soon as they walk through the door—workers may seem "switched off" and involved in their own private worlds. Even though some work is being done, it is performed as a drudgery. The visitor may feel that if he stood at the exit at one minute to five, he would likely be injured in the rush to escape.

Another sign of low motivation is voluntary absenteeism, which is increasing every year in most countries.

In summary, motivation is a question of energy and commitment. We all have untapped sources of energy that are not expressed because we do not see the value of committing ourselves. If we work for an organization that recognizes our worth and gives due weight and dignity to the time we spend working, then we will, naturally, give more of ourselves in return. This helps make the experience of working more fulfilling for each employee and more profitable for management.

REFERENCES

Herzberg, F. *Work and the nature of man.* New York: New American Library, 1973.
Maslow, A. H. (Ed.). *Motivation and personality* (2nd ed.). New York: Harper & Row, 1970.

Suggested Activities for Blockage 5—Low Motivation

Blockage 6 — Low Creativity

> *We have come to the point in biological history*
> *where we are now responsible for our own evolution.*
> Abraham Maslow

There was a time not so long ago when it was necessary to learn only one trade or profession in a lifetime, and the knowledge and skills a man acquired in his youth were still relevant on his retirement day. This, however, is no longer the situation. Some industries, like electronics engineering, face a continual and often bewildering rate of change that demands constant effort to keep up with current practices. Many other trades are less influenced by change, but only a few are totally free of innovation (horse breaking and dog training are the only ones we can think of on the spur of the moment).

Organizations and individuals live in a world of constant flux that comes from numerous sources—politics, society, education, technology; the list is virtually endless. Any organization that wishes to survive and grow needs to keep up with these trends and changes.

Consider the patterns of our economy. There is a decline in the number of people employed in manufacturing and an increase in the number employed in service industries. There is a move toward mass production and mass marketing. Products are less permanent, and some designs have built-in obsolescence. Jobs that are particularly dirty, hot, noisy, or unsatisfying tend to remain unfilled, despite local unemployment. Many young people reject accepted practices, absenteeism steadily increases, people retire sooner, and industrial conflicts have much of the bitterness and violent antagonism of a stifled rebellion. All these changes represent a challenge to our present practices; yet, to survive, we need to keep ahead by generating new ideas and practices—by being *creative*.

True creativity depends on being in close touch with the present situation and being able to battle against all that is repetitive, mechanical, and insensitive in our make-up. This demands a quality and depth of work that is hard to achieve. The computer, which surpasses man in many ways, is a cumbersome idiot when something new has to be generated. This is the unique contribution of man—his sensitivity, flexibility, and creative spark. These qualities can easily be stunted and destroyed by clumsy handling, but they are fundamental to every successful achievement.

In practice, creativity is often difficult because it challenges the established order and replaces certainty with uncertainty. Because people often fear this, you may hear comments like "better the devil you know than the devil you don't." In addition, the creative person, more often than not, makes mistakes and is often criticized for being unable to sort out the bizarre from the practical. However, if each new idea were censored before being expressed, in all likelihood it would go through such an obstacle course that its potential value would never be known.

One of the calamities of our age is the way we have developed industrial organizations without taking the human factor sufficiently into account. Millions of jobs have been designed to give minimum challenge and personal satisfaction to workers. No wonder there is so much disillusion in industry when we are surrounded by such ugly circumstances. The alternative is to use the creative potential of individuals and so bring about improved personal satisfaction, more enterprise, and a deeper understanding of the effects of business on the quality of life as a whole.

Because there are many forces working to inhibit creativity, we must consciously try to neutralize them and enable this untidy but vital creative process to flourish.

THE UNCREATIVE ORGANIZATION

The uncreative organization works like a machine—perhaps a very well-constructed and well-maintained machine, or perhaps a creaking, slow, and ill-designed device. Nevertheless, it is a machine, whose parts interact in completely predictable ways.

The managers spend little time developing new ideas for the future and pay only lip service to the importance of forward-looking ideas from employees. When someone does have an unusual idea, it is given a cold reception, unless it comes from the boss, whose notions are accepted without question. Others learn that it is safer not to "rock the boat."

People in uncreative organizations often learn that taking risks is dangerous and unrewarding. If it is the company's custom and practice to condemn every failure with gleeful malice, then people (especially managers) will be scared to do anything that involves uncertainty. As a result, managers stop having new ideas.

This can take root at every level. For top managers, it means that decisions about finance, marketing, and products are excessively conservative, protracted, and half-hearted. At lower levels, no one seems concerned to reorganize the stockroom or to simplify a particular document.

The effect of such creative constipation is slow growth and the likelihood that a competitor will take another jump ahead of you. Carried to extremes, the uncreative organization is a dying organization, one that has lost contact with the application and energy of its founders, that mechanically repeats old patterns, and that ceases to meet the needs of its customers. Such an organization, like the dinosaur, will rapidly become extinct.

THE OVERCREATIVE ORGANIZATION

You will not find many of these, but it is worthwhile to describe what happens when creativity is taken to excess.

Sometimes there is such a high value placed on new ideas that people spend all their energy thinking up new things without putting them to the test. Endless possibilities and lines of inquiry are opened up, but the ideas stay at a rather rarified and abstract level, and no one knows how to get things moving. Eventually, the organization collapses into impotence because it cannot choose between its many possibilities.

HOW TO BE CREATIVE

Creativity is a delicate plant—more like an orchid than a cabbage—and it needs the right atmosphere and conditions to flourish. In the right environment new ideas and risk taking are welcome and rewarded, and high-quality work can be performed.

Initially, there is a need to break away from old habits and routines and to extend our range of thinking so that all sorts of unconnected ideas can come together in unpredictable ways. The surfeit of ideas that often results must then be evaluated, selected, and developed.

Applying new ideas, like creating them, is a test of management competence. Even a brilliant thought needs to be developed and used before it becomes valuable.

Creative Characteristics

Creative individuals or groups tend to have the following characteristics.

- They are relaxed and open in their dealings with each other.
- They strive to create excellence, simplicity, and meaning in their work.
- They can handle many ideas and large amounts of information without being overwhelmed.
- They try not to program their minds in advance; rather they open their thoughts and allow ideas to develop.

In many ways, it is much easier to devise logical systems and to program people to work within them than to be truly creative, open, and flexible. Creativity takes courage. Yet both creativity and order are necessary; the problem is one of balance and relationship. The organization needs to respect both the creative and the routine, to enable both to flourish, and to provide them with ways of interrelating for the benefit of the whole.

Suggested Activities for Blockage 6—Low Creativity

Blockage 7 — Poor Teamwork

> United we stand,
> divided we fall.
> Aesop

Organizations exist to do complex tasks that no single individual could handle alone. Even if one man had lived ten thousand years, he could never have reached the moon unaided or sold Coca-Cola throughout the world. Working together in groups is enjoyable and personally satisfying for most people. Together, a team can accomplish much more than the total individual efforts of its members.

Psychologists have found that all teams have a tendency to follow certain rules. When a team is well led and meets the needs of its members, it tends to channel greater energy into effective work. On the other hand, a badly led team that frustrates its members expends a great deal of productive energy grumbling and retaliating.

People quickly recognize poor teamwork: the job never gets done properly, and bickering and lethargy develop among teammates. A poor management team results in widespread evils—chiefly, unhelpful competition, lack of integration, forgotten objectives, and a sullen sense of the impossibility of making progress.

"Building" a team is the result of much careful development by an overseer of the group. A supervisor (which in Latin means gardener) must "tend" his team with considerable effort and care. Like gardening, building a team involves responding to the seasons, meeting the needs of each "plant," and keeping the balance of the whole in mind.

This is recognized by the most talked-about managers of all—the sports-team managers—who put tremendous effort into creating a climate in which each player respects himself and still focuses his energies on the team's performance. The effect of such efforts by teammates is to multiply the resourcefulness of the team many times. In the hands of a brilliant manager who knows how to utilize the talents of his group, a no-chance, second-rate team can topple first-rate giants and be the best of the best.

Robert Townsend, author of *Up the Organization*, tells this story about his first day as the new chief executive of Avis, which had been consistently losing money in the past. The outgoing chief executive told Townsend that he would first have to fire all his managers. Three years later, the company had made ten million—but with exactly the same people (BBC film *Up the Organization,* 1973).

Some managers just seem to have a knack for building their people into an energetic, working team; others create mean and dull groups that avoid facing issues and that spend precious time backbiting and passing the buck. Even a manager himself may not realize what he does that is so valuable or destructive. But the process of building better work teams can be learned.

A successful team leader is, above all, true to himself. He is clear about standards, yet willing to give great trust and loyalty to his team, even during rough times. He also has the personal strength to maintain the integrity and position of his unit. Especially important is the need to be receptive to people's needs, and to pay attention to their hopes and dignity.

Because people usually cannot fight authority successfully, the style a manager adopts is a very important factor. Those of us who are responsible for leading teams have to make a serious choice about the way we manage, because whatever style we choose should reflect a deeply held personal belief. People quickly detect any attempt at role playing.

When we look at a management team, or at any other group or committee, there are two aspects of effectiveness that are more important than anything else: facing facts and establishing sound procedures. Although not easy, these two practices are essential for working effectively.

STAGES OF WORKING

Through experience, we have found that people go through the following stages in facing situations and developing their groups.

Stage 1—Initial Wariness

During this stage, personal feelings, weaknesses, and mistakes are covered up, and people are careful not to offer views that are contrary to the established line. No one cares much about others' views and there is no shared understanding about what needs to be done.

If the group remains at this stage, there is an increase in paperwork and in bureaucracy, people confine themselves to their own jobs, and the boss, not knowing what else to do, rules with a firmer hand. This may work satisfactorily if the boss has the wisdom, energy, and time to make the necessary decisions, but it is not teamwork in the real sense.

Stage 2—A Sorting-Out Process

If the members of the group (especially the senior person) want to face problems more openly, for the purpose of improvement and not punishment, then the group evolves toward a deeper level of working. As more personal and risky issues develop, people watch carefully to see whether they are punished for being bold. If problems can be discussed openly and without rancor, the group may become rather inward-looking and group members may become concerned about the views and problems of their colleagues.

In this stage, the team becomes open, but without further development it will remain somewhat inept, without the capacity to act in a unified, economic, and effective way.

Stage 3—Self-Organization

The group now has the confidence and trust in itself to take a fresh, rigorous look at how it operates and to devise new procedures for functioning more effectively. A more systematic, open approach develops which involves working through problems in a clear, energetic, and methodical way. Each of the following steps is followed in making decisions.

- **Clarifying the Purpose**—It has been said that a true fanatic redoubles his effort when he loses sight of his reason for action. We should never get so involved with the mechanics of working that we lose sight of our purpose. Effective teams are somewhat cynical, frequently asking, "What is this really going to do for us?"

- **Establishing the Objective**—It is one of the clichés of our era that objectives are important, although thousands of managers have witnessed the demise of management-by-objectives schemes under a soft cushion of red tape and empty phrases. Managers need to assign priorities and establish objectives for themselves in order to be really effective.

- **Collecting Information**—Decisions are made on the basis of information, opinion, and intuition. Experience painfully teaches us that if objective information precedes a decision, it is more likely to be a good one. This is part of the managerial trade. Just as a woodworker knows what has to be done to make a cabinet, so a successful manager knows what information is necessary to make a sound decision.

- **Considering the Options**—Generally, there are various ways of responding to a situation. As the saying goes, there are better ways of killing a cat than putting it tail first through a vacuum cleaner. When a group can generate all of its possible options before making a decision, the action will likely be more appropriate.

- **Detailed Planning**—Although it may seem expedient to act quickly, skipping the planning stage can lead to a great deal of wasted effort. Professional specialists exist to assist an organization in planning its work, but the fact remains that planning is an important skill that should not be subcontracted.

- **Reviewing from Experience**—Experience is one of the great teachers, but as someone pointed out, both the best and the worst flute players in the world learned their skills from experience. Practice or experience alone does not make perfect, but learning from experience can.

Stage 4—The Mature Team

After the "self-organization" stage has developed, there is a basis for a really mature team, with flexibility from a sound foundation as the keynote. Leadership is decided by the needs of the situation rather than by protocol, and energies are used for the benefit of the team as a whole.

Further, at this stage of development the team is concerned with thinking through the basic principles and responsibilities of management, including commercial, economic, and social aspects.

It is also necessary to make plans for the continual development of the group, recognizing that we live in a changing world in which inactivity inevitably means sterility and decay.

Contrary to popular belief, all individuals and groups are capable of development. The investment of time and effort in purposefully developing teamwork results in a very precious resource—being able to work together. The success of any enterprise depends on this ability.

Suggested Activities for Blockage 7—Poor Teamwork

Blockage 8 — Inappropriate Management Philosophy

> *This above all: to thine own self be true,*
> *And it must follow, as the night the day,*
> *Thou canst not then be false to any man.*
> Shakespeare

In a resort town on the coast, there is a large old hotel that caters mainly to tourists and business conventions. One of the waiters, a foreigner who has not really mastered the English language, tends to get confused at times, especially when the dining room is very busy. As a result, not only do customers often have to wait a long time for their food, but when it eventually does arrive, it turns out to be fish instead of steak, or Worcestershire sauce instead of tartar sauce. Watching how customers cope with that waiter is an education in itself. A few turn purple and bang and shout and generally insult him. A few others, who seem to understand his problem, try patiently to communicate or call over another waiter, who looks as if he could speak English. The rest, by far the majority, do not seem to know what to do, so they sit and eat their fish and Worcestershire sauce without comment or complaint.

Whenever people face challenges, they generally respond in one of three ways:

1. By fighting, like the people who shouted at the waiter. Unfortunately, in this case, the only result was to get the waiter more confused, and the people doing the shouting probably got so incensed that anger spoiled their meal.

2. By ducking or not facing the issue, like the people who accepted their fish and Worcestershire sauce. This type of response makes for an apparently quiet, amiable existence but it does not solve any underlying problems, which may accumulate and eventually overwhelm the passive avoider.

3. By trying to work constructively on the problem, like the few who patiently tried to communicate or called over an English-speaking waiter. These were the people who eventually solved their problem and got the right food.

If we look around, we see examples of managers behaving and responding in ways very similar to the challenges and problems that they face in everyday life.

When a manager fights, he tends to turn the situation into a trial of strength, or into a win-lose situation. If he wins regularly, he becomes strong and influential. The losers, on the other hand, creep away to lick their wounds and learn to avoid future confrontations. Managers who fight this way use fear to get things done. In the short term, results are often quite good, but they depend on the ability, ideas, and capacity of one man. In the long run, though, others find their own ways of avoiding delicate areas by walking on safe ground. With no one willing to take a risk, the potential contribution that employees can make is never harnessed, and, as a result, the organization loses.

When a manager ducks an issue, he is really doing the organization a disservice. If he continues to sweep problems under the carpet, or, like an ostrich, to bury his head in the sand and pretend the problems are not there, he is helping those problems get larger and larger. Unlike the manager who fights, this manager will not usually be feared, but neither will he be respected. And, because he does not face issues, people will not usually bring them up.

When a manager tries to work constructively on issues, people are much more likely to raise their own problems and ideas with him, thus maximizing everyone's contribution. This way of working really offers the best prospect of using the hidden potential of people.

Assumptions About Human Nature

Most constructive firms place a high premium on a management philosophy that encourages openness, probing, honesty, and a desire to face problems and to work constructively on solving them. But this can succeed only if the attitudes and beliefs of the people who work for the organization also reflect the same management philosophy. This relates to our evaluations of other people and our assumptions about their nature.

Because these matters are more a question of deep feeling than of superficial thought, some managers, not surprisingly, see them as more relevant to the psychiatrist's couch than to the board room. But many individual managers and organizations have found it extremely beneficial to consider their own fundamental beliefs as they relate to their management philosophy.

To accomplish this, we use a straightforward idea developed by Douglas McGregor, who found that the behavior a manager exhibited told a great deal about the way he valued other people and the assumptions he made about them (McGregor, 1960).

Managers in the first camp shared a view about people that McGregor called "Theory X." They believed that people:

- were fundamentally lazy and had to be pushed to work;
- were basically sly and interested only in their own benefit;
- responded best when disciplined and controlled;
- took notice of punishment and worked harder because of it;
- were essentially not interested in their jobs and worked against their will.

The other camp, "Theory Y," took a diametrically opposed view. They believed that people:

- were fundamentally willing to work on meaningful tasks;
- were basically honest and interested in the welfare of the group to which they belonged;
- responded best when given responsibility and some freedom to make their own decisions;
- took notice of honest praise and resented excessive punishment;
- were essentially interested in the quality of their professional and personal lives.

Now, of course, no manager is totally Theory X nor totally Theory Y, but the important finding that came out of McGregor's research was that those managers who tended to hold Theory-Y viewpoints were generally more successful in the following ways:

- Their departments had higher outputs.
- Their people showed more innovation.
- They had fewer labor problems.
- They had lower labor turnover.
- They had less waste.
- They achieved greater profits.

This research has led many organizations to explore more thoroughly their management philosophy and consciously to try to approach a Theory-Y style of operation. Experience has shown that this attempt can take place only if sufficient time and energy are invested; lip service is not enough. Any change has to be demonstrated in practice, through individuals. Although the Theory-Y approach is not without risk, the end product can be a much happier, healthier organization.

SOCIAL AND HUMAN RESPONSIBILITY

Even though the social responsibility of organizations is a fashionable subject today, it is still genuinely significant. Especially relevant to managers is the effect of business decisions on human communities and on the natural world.

Some businesses and other organizations have used their resources to reduce pollution, serve the community, assist social problems and conflicts, give responsible service to consumers, aid stable economic patterns, provide healthy conditions for employees, structure work to aid psychological satisfaction, support those in difficulty, and prepare individuals for the challenges of the future.

Creation of wealth for its own sake is a highly questionable and shallow aim. The question must be asked, "Wealth for whom and for what purpose?" and, perhaps more basically, "What is wealth?"

These are fundamental questions that must be asked by everyone with power and responsibility. The answers are far from easy, but the fact that they are debated leads to a deepening of management quality.

REFERENCE

McGregor, D. *The human side of enterprise.* New York: McGraw-Hill, 1960.

Suggested Activities for Blockage 8—Inappropriate Management Philosophy

Blockage 9 — Lack of Succession Planning and Management Development

*Nobody plans to fail
but many fail to plan.*

Some organizations seem to run like clockwork: there are always enough people around with the capacity to handle a bigger job when circumstances demand, and they do so without fuss or disaster; and the general level of performance meets the expectations of top management.

Although these utopian organizations are few and far between, a close inspection of them reveals that they give careful attention to two things: preparing for the future and developing each individual's capabilities.

Most organizations somehow seem to stumble through their succession and development problems, even without careful plans. Although too much planning can often lead to more problems, it is important to determine the degree of planning that is relevant.

One firm we know suddenly came face to face with a big succession problem. It operated over one hundred retail shops, most of which were managed by people in their fifties. When these managers first came into the business, retailing was seen as a good job, and young people were eager to enter the business. Only when these managers began to retire did the firm suddenly realize that it had a problem. For years the firm had not attracted people of the right caliber, nor had it projected future demand for managers. As a result, it soon had difficulty finding people of management potential from the present staff.

To help solve the problem, a keen training officer was hired to set up what he called a management-trainee scheme. Merrily, he recruited young men with college educations, promised them early appointments as store managers, and invested a lot of effort and money in their training. After two years, these trainees were ready for their first management appointments. Unfortunately, the results did not work out very well. During those few years, the pattern of retailing had begun to change: small shops were giving way to larger, self-service stores, bigger shopping centers serving wider areas were being opened, and the firm was now faced with redundant managers. Any talk of appointing the newly prepared trainees to management positions brought a swift and volatile reaction from existing managers, and the scheme understandably crumbled.

This example provides both a case *for* future planning and a case *against* it. At first, the firm had a problem because it did not plan for the future; then it had a problem because it did.

Unfortunately, there is always a case for and a case against future planning. The case *for* is based on three main arguments.

1. Future planning can help identify likely "people gaps" in the future. This knowledge will allow the time and effort necessary to train and develop employees.

2. It helps sort out who, within the firm, can be developed to a higher position. It is nonsense to develop people without a clear view of what they are being developed for, and, if you are not careful, you could find yourself developing people for your competitors.

3. If people know they have a good future with you, they are more likely to stay.

The case *against* future planning is based on two principal arguments.

1. It can lead to decisions being made too far ahead of time, like the firm mentioned earlier. Thus, if the situation changes, you could be left committed to the wrong horse.

2. By saying who is likely to get ahead in your firm, you are also, by default, saying who is likely to remain at the same level. Almost nothing we know turns people off faster than letting them know that they have no future.

On the whole, though, succession planning is usually worthwhile, because people in a firm inevitably change from time to time. It is better to have an inadequate plan, than no plan at all.

To provide for succession planning, a firm needs to know:

- Who is likely to leave (retirements, etc.) and what will happen when he does. This is especially important for key jobs.

- Who is likely to be promoted and what needs to be done to train him.

- Which jobs will likely need external recruitment.

To be effective, however, the plan should always be flexible and tentative—and employees should know this.

There was a time when personal development for managers meant that they were always packing their suitcases to go elsewhere, and this was seen as the answer to succession problems. Recently, though, there has been a reverse reaction. Management-succession problems are very difficult, and management-development specialists are still trying to find solutions and answers.

Frequently, those people who are most effective, energetic, and creative have little time for consultants, books, and formal training courses. They see that ability and knowledge are only valuable when put to practical use. Accumulating management skills is only one step; it is much more difficult to apply them. As Barry Goodfield, a psychologist friend of ours, puts it, "Insight without action produces anxiety."

Therefore, on the one hand we are saying that planning is important; on the other hand, if we plan to the extent that we remove the need for human judgment, then the system has a nasty tendency to become the master and not the servant. People need to be developed to meet the future needs of the organization, but real development is a result of increasing personal strength, judgment, energy levels, and adaptability.

Some organizations and individual managers, who feel uncomfortable with the fine words and neat systems beloved by personnel specialists, recognize all this from experience. They have created opportunities for real growth among people and have reaped the reward by having organizations that are alive and healthy and that constantly have a supply of promotable people.

If you want to establish a formal management-development and succession system, there are many manuals and well-tried methods available. Unfortunately, many people find that certain procedures cloud the situation and that paperwork inhibits action. Whatever method you employ, it is necessary to satisfy yourself that the system you choose will meet your organization's real development needs. (See also "A Word of Caution About Planning," in Blockage 10—Unclear Aims.)

Suggested Activities for Blockage 9—Lack of Succession Planning and Management Development

Blockage 10 — Unclear Aims

*A great deal of energy is spent on
work which is completely unnecessary.*
G. I. Gurdjieff

An organization that does not have a clear understanding of what it wants to achieve in a given time is like a ship without a rudder—at the mercy of the elements and likely to flounder in the first storm it meets.

Only by knowing what you want to achieve will you be able to decide on the action necessary to bring it about, yet time and time again we see firms that have no clear idea of where they are going. Some struggle for years complaining about economic conditions, resisting any kind of change, and wondering why their share of the market gets less and less. If they do expand, it is by accident or due to expediency.

The shop that is no longer located at the main shopping center, the garage that remains on what was once a major highway but is now a minor secondary road, and the manufacturer who uses yesterday's materials and methods because he is intimidated by technological change are all examples of organizations that did not think ahead. Very few firms have a far-reaching, progressive plan that is understood and approved by all members of senior management, or managers who really get the opportunity of voicing their opinions on where the firm should be heading.

It is not too difficult, with knowledge and experience, to establish a business that is reasonably successful, but the real test of sound business management comes when external factors change and affect the firm—when the shopping center moves, when there is decreased demand for the product being manufactured, or when competition presents itself. The organization that looks ahead, foresees difficulties, seizes opportunities, and learns how to redefine its aims in the light of changing circumstances is the one that gets bigger and better.

Very often, we spend too much time considering what is the best way of doing something and far too little considering what it is we really ought to be doing. Every now and then we should stop trying to devise more efficient ways of producing "widgets" and ask ourselves whether we should be producing them at all. To this end, many firms now develop corporate planning systems or hire planning consultants, but as one friend of ours puts it, "It's just a simple question of knowing where you're heading."

When it comes down to the performance of individuals or teams within an organization, the results of unclear aims are just as easy to see. One of the main reasons for low personal achievement is that individuals have no clear idea of the kind of performance that is required.

When a manager and his subordinates do not share a clear understanding of what is expected, the results can often turn sour. The manager makes false assumptions about his subordinate's ability and judges him by measures different from those he applies to himself. The subordinate's efforts are misplaced, he is judged unfairly, and, naturally, he becomes frustrated and dissatisfied. In the worst cases, the subordinate can work really hard but all the time be heading in the wrong direction. In the end neither he nor the firm benefits. It is not unreasonable for everyone in a position of responsibility to know what is expected of him and also to have the opportunity of discussing these expectations. In the same way, of course, it is important for the boss to understand the feelings and aspirations of his subordinates.

One of the chief inhibitors to achieving this mutual understanding is the gap between organizational and personal objectives. The organization may think it employs a manager simply to manage his department effectively, but the manager may have his own ideas about what he wants to achieve. In all probability, he wants to be recognized and to have the kind of job that leaves him enough time and energy to enjoy his nonworking life to the fullest. No one pretends that organizational and personal objectives are in complete accord, but, in truth, the closer they are, the happier and more effective the manager.

Another difficulty is our habit of seeing performance in input rather than in output terms. In other words, we tend to measure a man by the way he acts rather than by what he achieves. Right or wrong, people are judged by how they dress, whether they make quick decisions, whether they are late for work, or even whether their desk is tidy, rather than by the results they turn in. Even in job descriptions we find phrases like "he administrates," "he organizes," "he reports," "he coordinates." Until these descriptions are written in output rather than in input terms, they can help to inhibit rather than to develop management performance. As one renowned manager remarked, "Job descriptions are strait jackets," and any manager who is worth his salt will write his own job description anyway.

In recent years, researchers, having recognized the importance of clear aims, have developed a number of theories and training packages to help with the problem. Perhaps the most commonly known is "Management by Objectives."

The basis of most of these approaches is that a manager and his subordinate agree on what is reasonable to expect, how long it should take to achieve, and what measures will be used to assess performance. It is also important, of course, actually to assess performance and to use the experiences of the past to make better decisions about the future.

Experience shows that these approaches bring the greatest benefit when people work on their own initiative, without close supervision or support from above, e.g., the field-based salesman, the branch manager, or the holder of a key, influential job.

The ground rule is—the more important the job, the greater the need for clear aims.

Conversely, these approaches tend to be less useful when jobs are largely repetitive or when people work with close supervision or support.

A WORD OF CAUTION ABOUT PLANNING

Plans and discipline can be invaluable, but often good intentions simply do not bring material results. We have looked at some of the reasons why planning tends to be ineffective, and we were not surprised to find that there are certain obstacles that strangle effort and effective planning.

- **Management Indifference**—This occurs when managers fail to support and participate in the planning process, which often occurs when planning is forced on them. Ultimately, unless a plan clearly affects the decision-making process, it is seen as irrelevant and it withers away.

- **Unrealistic Expectations**—This develops when managers somehow expect the plan to take effect overnight and to revolutionize the company. Planning is a continuous process, and it takes time to learn how to handle it with maturity and depth.

- **Defensive Conservatism**—This occurs when management is unprepared to reorganize resources on the basis of the plan. There needs to be an interaction between the plan and the systems within the organization.

- **Incompetent and Irrelevant Planning**—Larger companies often employ professional planners, and smaller companies frequently subcontract a manager to undertake analysis and planning. When these people are weak, indecisive, or untrained, little of quality can emerge. A more subtle difficulty is unrealistic planning, often produced by eager and idealistic "whiz kids." Sometimes a work of business artistry is produced, but people feel that there is too great a gap between the vision of the plan and the reality of the situation.

- **Unclear Plans**—A clear vision of the "castle in the clouds" must be supported by a realistic and precise description of the routes and pathways that lead to utopia. Vague strategies, policies, or operating plans mean that the energy for change becomes dissipated in idealistic imagination, and little of consequence is achieved.

- **Ivory-Tower Planning**—An excellent plan with well-defined objectives and action steps can still fail if the plan—produced by a small, insular group—overlooks the traditions and perceptions within the organization and thus fails to gain commitment.

Suggested Activities for Blockage 10—Unclear Aims

Blockage 11 — Unfair Rewards

> *Companies that pay peanuts*
> *get monkeys.*
> Anon.

It would be much easier if we could talk about the human aspects of organizations without mentioning rewards—salaries, wages, and the other things people get in return for their effort—because many of our rewards are inequitable, and we have very few scientific methods of assessing how much people are worth. Some organizations pay the "trade-union rate," others have "job grading" or "incentive" schemes, and some just pay what they can get away with. But it is not only a question of how much a job is worth to the organization. When we discuss rewards we are talking about the total distribution of wealth in a society and the sharing of the national cake. These arguments, of course, are often political as well as economic.

Organizations need people, and people need organizations. By and large, the best people tend to go to the organizations offering the best rewards. Conversely, organizations that pay below par tend to get inadequate employees.

Money is an emotional subject because a person's financial position in our society is the benchmark of success. While we can avoid being judged on some aspects of our lives, our status at work is not one of them. We are constantly being assessed, graded, and categorized, and the position we hold is one of the main criteria by which others judge us. Like it or not, employers make a tangible decision about our worth, from which spring many consequences affecting and influencing our whole life style—the kind of house we live in, the type of car we drive, and even the educational opportunities for our children. We judge ourselves by our salary and status level and often measure success by the speed at which we climb toward the apex of the pyramid. This desire to get nearer the top is one of the main drives that give direction, challenge, and energy to our working lives.

Rewards, like coins, have two sides, and on the obverse is the less-pleasant reality of punishments. In a way, the absence of rewards is perhaps the main punishment that organizations can apply. Behavior that is valued by those with power is rewarded with higher material rewards and increased prestige; behavior that is less valued leaves people relatively deprived of these things. Achieving equity in this balancing act is often very difficult.

Many organizations have a complex web of negotiating procedures, committees, appraisal schemes, agreements, and the like for dealing with inevitably complex decisions concerning:

- **Wage Differentials**—Should Harry get more than Tom, and, if so, how much more?

- **Status**—Who should be paid by the hour, and who should have "staff" status?

- **Motivation**—Are we paying enough for people to commit their energy?

- **Social Responsibility**—What do we do about old Joe now that he is disabled?

- **The Disadvantaged**—Should we give more help to minority or other less-powerful groups?

- **Division of Labor**—Does our payment system prevent work from being organized in the optimum way?

- **Rigidity**—Are we sufficiently open to new ideas and concepts about rewards? Are we moving with the times?

- **Trade Unions**—Should we encourage or discourage trade unions? What should our negotiating tactics be?

When there is an inadequate framework for dealing with these kinds of decisions, managers frequently find themselves confused, depressed, and even mildly hysterical about the reward system. Often, they feel defensive and threatened, especially when workers are organized and potentially strong. As a result, decisions are made in response to threats, a course which inevitably breeds more inequity and more militancy.

Perhaps the crux of the dilemma is the conflict between the interests of the organization and those of the individual. Ideally, every organization would like to have a labor force that comprises only fit and able people who are willing and strongly motivated to serve the interests of the organization intelligently and resolutely, often to the comparative exclusion of their other interests. However, not everyone has either the desire or the capacity to match that kind of specification. People are more than just workers—they are husbands, wives, parents, church members, Boy Scout and Girl Scout leaders, members of the local sports team, and even chairmen of local dog-owners clubs—and there is more to life than just the organization. Some of us may be old, sick, unintelligent, dull, and rebellious, but we still have to live, eat, and work. Our contribution may be less important, but we do have something to give, and we need to feel that we are being rewarded adequately even though our contribution may be less than someone else's. (See also Blockage 5—Low Motivation.)

Logically, it could suit the organization's needs to reward the strong and to let the weak become someone else's burden. To some extent this happens in practice, but employee organizations and management's emotional unwillingness to confront situations are two big preventive barriers. Like it or not, we will never have the perfect "meritocracy." However, we still need to make decisions about the relative worth of our people.

Although there are many forces at work and no right answers, a clear policy should emerge and be tested in the day-to-day skirmishes of the factory, office, or laboratory. The organizations in the worst shape are those whose managers do not confront issues and, instead, let other forces make their decisions for them.

SYMPTOMS OF INADEQUATE REWARDS

If you recognize the following symptoms, rewards could be an issue in your organization.

- The wage system prevents work from being organized in an optimum way.
- Large numbers of people feel undervalued.
- Decisions about pay are forced on you.
- You get people with inadequate skills.
- There is an absence of machinery for dealing with issues about rewards.
- The reward system inhibits constructive change.
- You are not seen as a "good employer" in the locality.

Fortunately, money is not the only way in which people measure their value. Sufficient cash will not in itself achieve the high level of motivation needed by every dynamic and successful organization, but it will prevent a person from feeling grossly undervalued.

Suggested Activities for Blockage 11—Unfair Rewards

part four

Working on Clearing Your Blockages

Using the Activities

When a machine breaks down, it is usually possible, by following a logical process, to find out exactly which fault is causing the trouble. But people are not machines. With people, it is often much more difficult to determine exactly what is going wrong, and still more difficult to solve it.

Initially, we may have vague feelings that all is not well, but we cannot put a finger on either the problem or the solution. To compound the uncertainty, other people probably have different perceptions about what needs to be done, and, in the confusion, no one is quite sure what to do next.

Now that you have read those essays on the blockages that are relevant to you and to your business, you may have a fairly clear idea of what you would like to change. The fifty activities that follow are designed to help you proceed. Therefore, this section of *People at Work* is perhaps the most important because it describes specific ways to do something about the blockages that you may have in your organization.

The activities are intended to be useful to those who, by reading the earlier chapters, have found problems on which to work and also to those who, as yet, are unable to clarify exactly what problems exist. Some of the activities are directly concerned with solving problems, but the majority are designed to help you better understand the nature of your problems. We believe that, in most cases, clarifying the nature of problems is the single, most important step on the way to solving them. When a capable manager knows and understands what problems he has, he can usually find the solutions himself.

There is another important reason for designing the activities this way. We want them not only to help solve problems but to contribute to your personal development—which, we must re-emphasize, comes best from personal experience. One meaningful, practical experience is usually worth ten books on the subject!

All the activities can be used by both the experienced and the inexperienced. They are presented concisely and can easily be adapted to suit your own needs. If you are not familiar with the method of approach, it is best to stick closely to the instructions. As you become more experienced you will be able to devise your own variations that will better fit the circumstances in your organization.

To begin, choose an activity that deals with a particular problem you are facing. Or, you can begin with the activity "Starting Development Using *People at Work*."

Each activity has detailed, step-by-step instructions. The initiator should prepare himself carefully for those activities requiring pre-planning. Because many of the activities include meetings and discussion sessions, it is helpful to arrange suitable settings and facilities. We invite you to use the following check list when preparing for an activity.

1. Is the room sufficiently quiet?
2. Is the physical setting comfortable?
3. Can all interruptions be avoided?
4. Are there adequate supplies of flip charts, felt-tipped markers, paper, etc.?

Remember that it is important to take matters seriously and to provide proper facilities for the sessions. Understandably, the most common cause of failure is poor preparation.

Not only must the initiator, or facilitator, plan and prepare for an activity, he must also allow sufficient time for people to discuss their feelings. In effect, this means that he is responsible for seeing that data are openly discussed, evaluated, and integrated with participants' learnings. Since there is the possibility of emotional affect—stress, ambivalence, confusion—resulting from structured activities of this kind, the facilitator should be aware that such feelings need to be alleviated or resolved by an adequate discussion of the experience.

The following guidelines may help you.

- Allow at least twenty minutes for discussion at the end of the group activity.
- Watch for signs of discomfort in participants.
- Invite each person to fully describe his feelings.

The activities have been tested, so you can have confidence in their value. However, if you find that a group activity is unproductive, it is usually because either the topic is not of real concern to the group, or people do not feel able to work on the problem. In such a case it is important to find out why an activity fails and to take practical steps to remedy the situation. Until a group can work together on the issues that are important to the members, there is little chance of real progress.

Having written these cautionary notes, it simply remains to say that the activities are often fun and exciting. We hope you will find them so. Problems are serious, but seriousness can easily turn into a heavy, stodgy attitude to change. So enjoy yourself!

ACTIVITIES

This section contains a collection of fifty activities that we have found useful in helping people begin clearing the blockages in their organizations.

1   Starting Development Using PEOPLE AT WORK

Purpose

This activity is designed to help a team apply the approach of *People at Work* to its own work situation. A short workshop, it allows those who make decisions about the use of human energy in the firm to explore the ideas in the book and to decide what practical steps should be taken to put the ideas to use.

Participants

All those with responsibility or influence over the utilization of people in the firm are candidates, preferably as widespread and influential a group as possible. Some people may not be able to join initially for "political" reasons, but they should be involved as early and as fully as possible.

It is helpful, but not essential, for one participant to act as an observer. He takes no part in the activity except to watch how matters proceed. At the end of the session, the observer reports on what occurred during the workshop. For a more detailed idea of the observer's role, use activity 30, "Process Review," as a guide.

Materials

Paper, pencils, felt-tipped markers, masking tape, and a flip chart are needed.

Time and Setting Required

Two days is the best length of time for the workshop, although a one-day session makes a good start. The location should be removed from office concerns and telephones. A weekend retreat at a remote hotel is ideal.

Preparation

Two weeks prior to the workshop, ask each participant to read *People at Work* before he arrives. Participants should also have completed the Blockage Questionnaire in Part Two and computed their scores.

Process

1. On arrival, explain the format of the workshop, distribute several blank sheets of paper to each participant, and then ask each individual to write down what he or she would like to see emerge from the experience.

2. Each individual's aims and expectations are written on a flip chart (newsprint), posted on the wall, and shared by the whole group. After this sharing has taken place, the group identifies the three most significant points that were made. These points are posted separately and left on the wall during the sessions as a reminder of the general aims of the workshop. (This phase takes approximately ninety minutes.)

3. Ask everyone to submit his scores (anonymously, if preferred) on the Blockage Questionnaire. List the eleven blocks of the questionnaire on a flip chart and write the scores of each participant next to the corresponding block. Then compute the average scores for the group as a whole and pick out the two blockages that have the highest scores. The group can then decide whether the blockages with the highest scores are the most significant for the organization at the moment. If there is disagreement, the group discusses what it feels are the two primary blockages. (At least one hour should be allowed for this phase.)

4. Divide the group into pairs (an odd person can join any group) and ask each pair to list incidents that demonstrate the two primary blockages in the organization. (This phase takes at least one hour.)

5. When each pair's list is completed, the whole group reconvenes to discuss the lists. Concurrently, make a consolidated list of all the points and indicate particularly important ones by underlining. Then the entire group discusses the overall outlook and makes a new list of the six main points on which to work. (This takes approximately one hour.)

6. The group again divides into pairs and each pair works through the activities and text of *People at Work* to come up with a detailed list of suggestions for the organization's improvement. The list should specify what is to be done, who will be involved, what resources are needed, when the work is to be undertaken, and, most importantly, the purpose. (This phase takes about two hours.)

7. The whole group reassembles and discusses each pair's ideas, which are carefully listed on a flip chart. The group decides which

activities it wishes to try collectively. Then, the entire group or numerous subgroups can plan in more detail:

- What is to be done?
- Who is going to do it?
- How is it to be tackled?
- What resources are required?
- When is it to be reviewed?
- When is the next meeting of the group?

8. Following the collective-planning stage, ask each manager to spend an hour alone to consider his own situation and to decide what he wishes his department to accomplish.

9. At the final meeting of the whole group, the observer, if one was used, reports on the sessions. The whole group reviews and processes the experience and each manager shares with the group what he personally plans to tackle.

2   To Change or Not to Change

Purpose

Whenever a need for change is indicated, there will always be arguments both for and against the change. Such problems can often be tackled more rationally by using a method developed by Kurt Lewin called force-field analysis, which analyzes the forces working both for and against change (respectively, driving forces and resisting forces). This activity is designed to help you identify these forces, reduce the resisting forces, and increase the driving forces. If you follow this process your chances of bringing about the changes you require should be much improved.

Participants

The activity can be carried out individually, in pairs, or in groups.

Time Required

Approximately one hour.

Process

First, you need to select a problem that you feel you ought to do something about but that you do not know how to tackle. The activity is more useful if other people or groups also are involved in the problem. Use separate sheets of paper for notes and complete each step before going on to the next.

1. Identify the problem as you see it now and describe it in writing.

2. Now define the problem in terms of (a) the present situation and (b) the situation you would like to see when the problem is solved.

3. Make a list of the forces working against change (resisting forces). Then make a list of the forces working *for* change (driving forces). These forces can be people, finances, external factors, etc.—anything either inhibiting or enhancing your ability to reach a change.

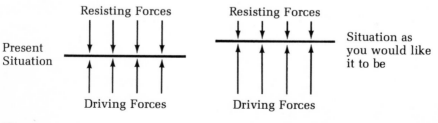

4. Underline those forces that seem to be the most important.

5. For each resisting force underlined, list the factors that could possibly reduce or eliminate the force.

6. For each driving force underlined, list the factors that could possibly increase it.

7. Determine the most promising action steps you could take toward solving your problem and the resources available to help you.

8. Re-examine your action steps and put them in sequence, omitting any that do not seem to fit in with your overall aims:

   Action Steps   When   How

9. Review the experience for its total effect and apply it to your problem.

3   First Impressions

Purpose

The activity is designed to examine how new people feel about your organization when they arrive.

Process

1. Give each of the next three people who are hired by your organization two sheets of paper that divide the following two days into thirty-minute intervals. Explain the purpose of the activity and ask them to note on the paper (1) where they are, (2) what they are doing, and (3) what they are feeling, for each half hour at work during the next two days. (See the Sample Diary Sheet.) Explain why the information is needed and assure anonymity. Also try to see that the new people are not treated specially.

2. When the three diary sheets are completed, examine them and list five improvements that could facilitate an employee's introduction into the firm.

3. Discuss these ideas with managers, supervisors, and other related personnel, and move toward a commitment to improve.

4. Repeat the activity if necessary with another set of new employees.

SAMPLE DIARY SHEET

Time	Where you are	What you are doing	What you are feeling
8:00			
8:30			
9:00			
9:30			
10:00			
10:30			
11:00			
11:30			
12:00			
12:30			
1:00			
1:30			
2:00			
2:30			
3:00			
3:30			
4:00			
4:30			
5:00			

4   Selection Interviews

Purpose

This activity is designed to help you see whether systematic selection practices can improve your organization's interviewing procedures.

Process

1. Call a meeting for all those who actually hire new people in your organization and ask them to utilize this systematic selection experiment on a trial basis when they recruit new employees.

2. Ask each interviewer to think about the vacant job in the following way: decide what essential qualities and what desirable qualities the new employee will need and write them down on the Systematic Selection Chart, then interview the applicant following each step of the chart, checking off each point as you proceed. When you have completed the chart, decide whether this more systematic way of hiring has any benefit for your organization.

3. When this method has been tried a few times, call another meeting and decide whether the procedure is considered beneficial by the group.

SYSTEMATIC SELECTION CHART

Qualities	Essential	Desirable
1. Physical		
Appearance		
Age		
Health		
Special		
2. Mental		
Intelligence		
Motivation		
3. Background		
Education		
Training		
Achievements		
4. Work Experience		
Relevant		
Stable		
5. Other Points		

5   Cost of Recruitment

Purpose

This activity will enable you to see how much it costs when you hire someone new.

Process

1. Write the names of the last three people you hired on a copy of the Cost of Recruitment Sheet.

2. Then find out how much it cost you to recruit each one of them. (This will require some detective work.) Make the figures as accurate as possible by asking your people to specify exactly what was involved.

    Remember to take into account the varying costs of the people involved in the hiring process. For example, you could compute executive time at $10 (or £3) an hour and nonexecutive time at $5 (or £1.50) an hour.

COST OF RECRUITMENT SHEET

	Most Recent Recruit		Second Most Recent		Third Most Recent	
	Name:		Name:		Name:	
	Time	Cost	Time	Cost	Time	Cost
Cost of His Predecessor's Departure						
1. Severance pay						
2. Loss of output (job vacancy)						
Cost of Recruitment						
1. Contacting employment agency						
2. Advertising						
3. Job specification						
4. Interviewing						
5. Considering choice						
6. Making offer						
Cost of Introduction						
1. Clerical costs on starting						
2. Time taken to achieve competence						
3. Time taken by people in training						
4. Loss of output during introductory training						

Total [   ]   Total [   ]   Total [   ]

6   Those Who Leave

Purpose

This activity can be used if you feel worried about what seems to be excessive or costly staff turnover. It attempts to discover facts about people who leave your organization. Because some detective work is again required to sort out the facts, this kind of project is a good development experience for a young, up-and-coming manager.

Process

1. On the Those Who Leave Worksheet we have listed categories of employees common to many organizations. To make the list more relevant to your own organization, add any categories that pertain to your type of business. Then check your records and, on a separate sheet of paper, list the name (or payroll number) of each person who was employed by your organization exactly twelve months ago and divide these people into their respective categories. Write the total number of people employed in each category in column A of the Those Who Leave Worksheet.

2. Check your records to see which of these people are still employed by your organization and which have left. Enter the number of persons in each category who have left in column B of the worksheet.

3. To determine the percentage of staff turnover for each employee category, complete the straightforward equation in column C of the worksheet.

4. When the percentage of staff turnover for each category has been determined, you can note the areas in which turnover seems to be a problem and try to find out why.

5. Further investigation could involve noting any differences between stayers and leavers (such as age, marital status, job status, qualifications, nationality, etc.).

THOSE WHO LEAVE WORKSHEET

	A Numbers Employed One Year Ago	B Numbers No Longer Employed	C Percentage of Staff Turnover $\frac{B}{A} \times 100$
Managers			
Supervisors			
Craftsmen			
Senior Operatives			
Salesmen			
Technicians			
Operators			

7 Team Interview

Purpose

This activity explores the benefits of a team approach to personnel selection.

Process

1. Choose a set of interviews in which it would be appropriate for three or four people to be involved in the selection process. This can be an actual interview or one conducted with "dummy" candidates.

2. Divide the interviewers into two teams.

3. Ask each team to interview the applicants and to arrive at a team selection.

4. When both teams have made a choice, bring them together to share their views and choices.

5. Discuss whether the team approach brought any advantages to the selection process and whether the final selection would have been the same had the normal selection procedure been followed.

6. Consider whether to recommend amendments to your normal selection process.

8 The Company Tree

Purpose

Designed to clarify the formal organization within your firm, this activity ascertains how various people see the organizational structure and their own positions within that structure. It also provides a basis for discussing different perceptions.

Explanation

The activity is based on an old parable about a group of blind men who come across an elephant in their travels.

One blind man felt the elephant's leg and said, "An elephant is like a tree."

The second blind man touched the elephant's ear and said, "You are wrong, an elephant is like a fan."

The third blind man, while touching the elephant's side, said, "You are both wrong. An elephant is like a wall."

The fourth blind man held the tail and said, "It is clear that none of you has any understanding. An elephant is like a rope."

Each man believed his perception was accurate, yet the true picture was a combination of viewpoints.

Process

Stage One

The senior managers or senior group in the firm meet to discuss their concepts of the organization's structure and lines of responsibility. They prepare a "company tree," or organization chart, which represents the management's perception of the formal organization within the firm. This chart may look like the example on the following page.

The chart is not circulated at this stage because the next step is to check the perceptions of others in the organization.

Stage Two

Duplicate sufficient copies of the Company Structure Sheet for each person on the Company Tree. Invite each related jobholder to complete the sheet and to return it to the senior manager or senior group, whoever organized the chart.

SAMPLE COMPANY TREE

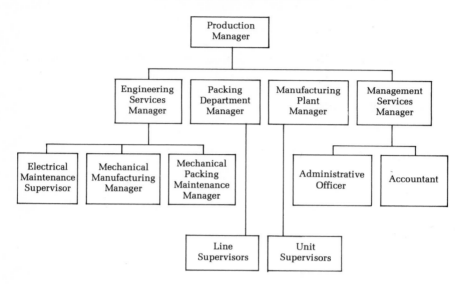

Stage Three

The senior people examine each Company Structure Sheet and compare it to their own perceptions of the Company Tree. At this time, oddities, misunderstandings, and erroneous conclusions are identified.

The senior group then discusses the following questions:

1. Are there any discrepancies or gaps in our organizational structure?

2. Is our present structure the best arrangement for us?

If any modifications in the company structure were made as a result of the discussion, the group compiles a final Company Tree.

Stage Four

A meeting is held for jobholders in the organization to clarify each person's position and to sort out "who-does-what" questions.

COMPANY STRUCTURE SHEET

Please fill out the answers below:

My job title:

The people I am responsible to:

The people I am responsible for:

My comments on our organizational structure are:

Signature _____ Date_____

9   Organization and People

Purpose

This activity is designed to expose the effect of your firm's organization on the employees.

If, after reading through the process, you feel that this approach would not work in your organization, it is likely that Blockage 8— Inappropriate Management Philosophy—will be useful to consider.

Process

1. Invite groups of people who normally work together—representing all levels of the business, i.e., from manager to receptionist—to form small discussion groups, and ask them to discuss the following questions.

   - What are the good features about the way the firm is organized now?

   - What are the bad features about the way the firm is organized now?

   - How could we improve the organization to help people work together more effectively?

2. Tell everyone honestly what you intend to do with the information, and also emphasize that at least two hours is optimal for them to consider the questions thoroughly. Appoint a recording secretary for each group to list the important suggestions.

   If this is the first time that you have asked your employees to contribute ideas of this kind, they will naturally be somewhat defensive and resistant at first. But open feedback from your co-workers can often reveal any number of useful, time-saving, and money-saving ideas about how things could be better accomplished.

   If your employees will not discuss problems that directly affect them, you probably have a closed and rigid organization. If this suits your firm and you like this type of environment, you may not want to change, even though a wealth of good ideas may be left fallow.

3. When several work groups have completed their lists for the questions, you have two options: you can either spend a day alone thinking about their points and deciding what you want to do; or (and this is the better option) you can list each group's notes with a felt-tipped marker on a flip chart, display all the sheets on the wall of

the meeting room, and invite your senior people to a two-hour meeting. At the meeting, explain that the views were received from employees in response to questions about the nature of your firm's organization. Ask the group to consider and discuss each point separately and to decide whether some action should be taken to improve the situation. Plan for a two-hour meeting each week until the group is satisfied that all matters worth consideration have been discussed.

10 Technology and Structure

Purpose

This activity will help determine the impact of your technology on the way your firm is organized and help you decide whether your form of organization is the most appropriate.

Process

1. Duplicate the Technology and Structure Chart and distribute copies to a selected review team, preferably heads of departments who have diverse viewpoints.

2. Ask each member of the team to complete the chart and to bring the completed sheet to a group meeting, where it will be the focus for discussion.

3. At the opening meeting, display the charts and discuss their implications. Ask each group member to produce a paper on one of the five questions listed at the end of the activity. If the group is large, a study team can be formed to deal with each question.

4. After a period of approximately six weeks, the review team meets again and the papers are read. Clear proposals should emerge, addressed to those with the power to influence the way the firm is organized.

TECHNOLOGY AND STRUCTURE CHART

Directions. You have a total of ten points for each vertical column. Read each description and see which type—A, B, C, or D—suits your own job most closely. Allocate the ten points to one or more descriptions as you see fit. When you have filled in the first vertical column, complete the same steps for the other three. Please complete and retain this chart in preparation for a group meeting.

DESCRIPTION OF THE WORK (i.e., technology)	Myself in My Job	My Work Group	My Department	My Company
TYPE A: Craft-oriented, project work. Some innovation, but not especially creative.				
TYPE B: Predictable, sometimes rather complex, repetitive, and continuous.				
TYPE C: Uncertain, rapidly changing, requiring high creativity and much risk.				
TYPE D: Giving service in which image, flair, and atmosphere are important.				
	Total: 10 Points	**Total:** 10 Points	**Total:** 10 Points	**Total:** 10 Points

TECHNOLOGY AND STRUCTURE QUESTIONS

1. How well does our organization fit the technology within which we operate?

2. Could we reorganize in a way that could increase people's contributions?

3. How differently should various departments be organized?

4. Are our units the wrong size to provide meaningful and satisfying work?

5. Does our management style meet the needs of our technology?

11 Organizational Options

Purpose

This activity is designed to examine the various possible forms of organization that are open to you, and to enable you to discuss possible changes.

Process

1. Get together a group of people who can influence the way the company is organized and distribute a copy of the Organizational Options Sheet to each member.

2. Ask each person to circle the number best representing the form of organization in your firm at the present time.

3. When the sheets are evaluated, try to compute a rough average for the group.

4. Then discuss, factor by factor, the merits of moving to the left or right for each item.

ORGANIZATIONAL OPTIONS SHEET

Instructions. Consider the organization as it is formed at the present time. Circle the number that you feel best represents the present state of affairs for each factor.

Centralization	1	2	3	4	5	Decentralization
Tall Pyramid	1	2	3	4	5	Squat Pyramid
Functional Structure	1	2	3	4	5	Integrated Units
Single-Line Authority	1	2	3	4	5	Matrix or Group Authority
Autonomous Units	1	2	3	4	5	Dependent Units
Individual Management	1	2	3	4	5	Collective Management
Clearly Defined Jobs	1	2	3	4	5	Flexible Jobs
High Creativity	1	2	3	4	5	Low Creativity

12 The Control Audit

Purpose

This activity is designed to help you determine whether decisions are being made at the right decision-making level and with adequate information.

Process

1. Ask each senior manager in your firm to complete a copy of the Management Control Questionnaire; then pool the answers.

2. Arrange a two-hour discussion meeting of all those involved.

3. Each manager can repeat the process with those who report to him, if he feels it is appropriate.

MANAGEMENT CONTROL QUESTIONNAIRE

Directions. This questionnaire is intended to collect some information and opinions about our management control systems—in particular, how decisions are made. You can help by giving some thought to the questions below. Answer each question from your own viewpoint, with as much openness and detail as you feel are appropriate. If there is not enough space on the questionnaire, continue on another sheet.

1. What activities are critical to our successful operation?

2. How well do our present control systems cope with each activity?

3. Give examples of as many incidents as you can remember of breakdowns in control.

4. What additional information do you need to do your job better?

5. Which functions have problems either of overload or lack of control?

6. What proposals would you make to improve the quality and effectiveness of control within the department (organization)?

13   Using Consultants

Purpose

Many managers are bombarded with alleged helpers, advisers, or consultants. Although the relationship between company and consultant often proves disappointing, sometimes the outcomes are invaluable. This activity will help you get maximum benefit from your investment in consultant help.

Process

1. Use Part A of the Consultation Check List at a management meeting to discuss whether outside help is required in a specific situation.

2. Part B should be worked through in relation to the consultants you are considering engaging.

CONSULTATION CHECK LIST

Part A—What Help Do We Need?

1. What is the problem?

2. Whose problem is it?

3. What are the symptoms?

4. What would happen if the problem went away?

5. How much does the problem cost us?

6. How much is it worth to solve the problem?

7. Can we solve the problem internally?

8. Do we need to learn how to tackle this kind of problem ourselves?

9. What objectives should we set for the consultant?

10. How can we use the consultant's skills to benefit our management development?

Part B—Discussion with the Consultant

1. What relevant experience does he have?

2. Is he really interested in understanding our problems?

3. Does he make us think and act differently?

4. Will he be acceptable to our people?

5. Does he set realistic objectives?

6. How are we going to judge success?

7. Who or what is going to be developed by the project?

8. What is the likely cost in terms of fees and effort on our part?

9. Whose interest is the consultant likely to follow—his or ours?

14   How Do We Control?

Purpose

This activity is designed to examine whether control is seen as inhibitive or supportive. It is a good activity for a work group, although it can be adapted to work within the organization as a whole.

Process

1. Duplicate the How Do We Control? Questionnaire and ask people to complete it privately.

2. Collect the scores and compute the average. If the average is more than 8, you could have control problems and should seriously consider working through a number of other activities to increase involvement.

3. Use the questionnaire again later to check how well you are progressing.

HOW DO WE CONTROL? QUESTIONNAIRE

Directions. This questionnaire is designed to help us see how much we feel over- or undercontrolled and whether we feel that we have sufficient personal control over our own work.

Answer each item by checking one of the boxes. Then add up the checks to get a total for each vertical column.

Each answer in the right-hand column counts as 2 points, each answer in the left column as 0 points. No answer—genuine indecision—counts as 1.

Who has responsibility for how I perform?	☐ I	☐ someone else
I would like to be controlled . . .	☐ more	☐ less
I would like to have conversations with my boss . . .	more ☐ often	less ☐ often
Control is the main function of management.	☐ false	☐ true
People work better when they are controlled . . .	☐ loosely	☐ closely
My boss delegates . . .	☐ adequately	☐ insufficiently
Decision making should be delegated more frequently.	☐ false	☐ true
I feel that I can do my job properly.	☐ true	☐ false
I feel an important part of the decision making in the firm.	☐ true	☐ false

I am clear about the
reasons why we do things.   ☐ true   ☐ false

⬜ Total

(0 points each)   (2 points each)

Add 1 point for each item not answered ⬜

TOTAL POINTS ⬜

Reveal only your total score. Keep individual answers to yourself unless you feel like discussing them.

15 Limits of Authority

Purpose

We sometimes find that managers, particularly middle managers and supervisors, actually make few independent decisions. If you suspect that this is the case within your organization, try this activity, which is designed to see if managers and supervisors actually make decisions or if they are simply responding to instructions from others.

Time Required

This activity is somewhat complex, and two and one-half hours should be allocated for each individual interviewed (this includes the time required to analyze the results).

Process

1. Begin at the top by interviewing the senior manager and list all the usual decisions he makes in an *average* week. List the exceptional decisions he makes on a separate page. Then code each decision with the following letters:

A	means full authority to act.
F	means full, but always delegated, authority to act.
A + R	means authority to act, but the manager must report his action.
R	means recommendation is required, but the manager has no real authority to decide.
NR	means no authority to act or recommend.
I	means irrelevant to the job.

2. After you have assigned a letter to each of the decisions the manager makes, add up the number of times each letter occurs and look at the proportions.

3. Continue the same procedure downwards through all management grades in the organization, level by level, until each has been covered.

4. Calculate the average for each level's decision-making profile. This information, when clearly expressed, forms an excellent basis for examining whether managerial positions are genuinely significant and meaningful within the organization.

16 Assessing Job Training Needs

Purpose

This activity provides a means to investigate a job that is either to be performed by a new person or is at present being done badly.

Process

1. Distribute copies of the Job Training Needs Sheet to all those employees who know about the job in question, such as the supervisor, the manager, the person responsible for giving the person his work, the recipients of the output, and, if possible, the actual jobholder.

2. When you have collected this information, you may find it is possible to develop a training plan.

   However, if the job is particularly difficult or important and there is no easy way of identifying what the jobholder must learn, you may find it necessary to use the services of someone who understands modern training methods, such as a training specialist, to sort out the problem. If possible, use someone within the organization; but if no one is readily available, investigate whether a consultant is needed by using activity 13, "Using Consultants."

JOB TRAINING NEEDS SHEET

Job Title:

Why does this job exist?

How do we know when the job is being performed well?

What tasks have to be done?

What does the jobholder have to learn to perform the job well?

17   Does Training Pay?

Purpose

This activity is designed to assess whether improved training would be a worthwhile investment.

Process

1. Gather together a group of about five managers to form a training evaluation group, at least two of whom should be hard-nosed production men who are used to saying what they think. Ask the group to choose a department in the organization that has the following three characteristics:

   - An improvement in people's performance would bring useful economic benefits.
   - The section is important to the success of the business.
   - The responsible manager is open to change.

   Ideally, the department chosen should have between ten and thirty people.

2. Once a department has been selected, invite three good training consultants to investigate the department and to submit test-case proposals. Discuss your plan with the consultants and emphasize that the proposal that seems most professional and thorough will be accepted.

   Before you let the consultants "loose," however, investigate the department yourself so that you will have a clear idea of what you want to achieve. Once you have a measure of the present performance of the section, you will be able to evaluate any variations from the norm.

3. Carry out the selected proposal and watch the department like a hawk for three months. Then evaluate the cost benefit of the activity. If the return investment exceeds 20 percent, the group could recommend how to spread planned training to other comparable departments and jobs.

18 Training Practice

Purpose

This activity is designed to discover how people feel about current training practices in the organization.

Process

1. Distribute a copy of the Learning Needs Questionnaire to each employee in your organization (or, if you have a large outfit, to a percentage of employees) and ask them to return the questionnaires anonymously. If you use a percentage of employees, make certain that it is a fully representative group—i.e., from managing director to typist.

2. Summarize the information on the completed questionnaires (if they are not returned, something is being said about the climate in the organization).

3. Circulate a copy of the data to each department head, and ask him to comment on the relevance of the results to his section.

4. You can then establish project groups to begin working on the important issues.

LEARNING NEEDS QUESTIONNAIRE

Directions. Circle the number that you feel best represents your experience.

I am not well prepared for my job.	1	2	3	4	5	I am fully prepared for my job.
I lack essential skills for my job.	1	2	3	4	5	I have all the necessary skills for my job.
I was not carefully introduced to my job.	1	2	3	4	5	I was carefully introduced to my job.
I found it difficult to learn my job.	1	2	3	4	5	I learned my job with minimal difficulty.
I have no opportunities for development.	1	2	3	4	5	I have good opportunities for development.
I have far too little proper training.	1	2	3	4	5	I have sufficient training.
My boss is not concerned about training needs.	1	2	3	4	5	My boss is concerned about training needs.

19   Improving Counselling

Purpose

This activity is designed to examine how well you help others develop their skills and knowledge.

Background

Research shows that most people display a need for five things in their working relationships.

1. *Safety Needs*—Securing, holding on to, protecting, and conserving the job as a source of livelihood.
2. *Friendship and Belonging Needs*—Satisfactory relations with colleagues and one's boss, commonly expressed as the need for belonging.
3. *Needs for Justice and Fair Treatment*—To be adequately rewarded for contributions in comparison with others.
4. *Dependence/Independence*—To be treated as a responsible adult, in whom needs for both dependence and independence are recognized.
5. *Needs for Achievement*—The opportunity to develop within the job and to realize one's potential to the fullest.

Process

1. Set up an informal, private meeting with each of your subordinates. Open the discussion by explaining that you want to learn more about how effectively you meet each person's real needs in the organization. Read the five needs listed under "Background" and, after allowing your subordinate time to consider them, discuss whether he feels that this is a realistic and useful list.

   Discuss each need separately and ask, "How well do you feel that this need is met here?" Encourage a free discussion and try to get an overall "feel" of the person's general level of satisfaction.
2. Decide what changes, if any, could facilitate greater satisfaction of the person's needs. Make a few specific agreements to foster change and see what happens.
3. Meet with each person again after six weeks and review whether anything useful has developed. Try to find ways of developing the relationship further.

20 The Job as a Motivation

Purpose

Job enrichment can easily be mishandled. Unless you are very careful, enriching one person's job may mean de-enriching someone else's. Although there is much to be gained from improving the psychological satisfaction of people at work, a slick formula can often create bitterness and rejection. Therefore, it is important to gain the acceptance of each level of employees, beginning with top management and working down.

This activity is designed to discover which aspects of a job produce positive or negative motivation in an employee, thus enabling you to begin work on enrichment without the threat and disturbance common to many such schemes.

Participants

The activity can be undertaken between any manager and one of his subordinates. It is applicable at any level—from manager to receptionist—and can be used as a kind of "do-it-yourself" job enrichment.

Process

1. Ask each person to look at his job description and to make sure that all the main aspects of his job are listed.

2. Then have him mark each aspect of his job with the letter A, B, C, D, or E, as follows:

    A—extremely satisfying
    B—quite satisfying
    C—somewhat satisfying
    D—not satisfying
    E—positively dissatisfying

3. After the individual has "graded" each item, ask him how the item could be improved so that it goes up at least one grade on the scale.

4. Positive effort should be devoted to those aspects that are given a D or an E rating to see what makes them so unrewarding. Then consider whether the tasks could be automated, reorganized, or changed in some way.

21   The Extra Push

Purpose

Every individual and group can call on reserves of energy in times of special need. This activity will help you discover whether your people are able and willing to give this extra push. The goal is to review experiences and to find out, in practice, how much effort was actually produced when needed.

Participants

This method can be used either with a group of people who usually work together or with representatives from different parts of your organization.

Process

1. Arrange a meeting of the selected group and ask each member to come prepared with a case history of the last special effort demanded by the organization. This case history should specify what caused the problem, how the problem was perceived, and how people responded to it.

2. At the meeting, write all the reported incidents on a flip chart and decide which one was most critical.

3. Then explore the most critical incident by asking:
   - Who was involved?
   - How did they respond?
   - How much additional effort was given?
   - What effort could have been offered but was not?
   - Could this special effort be used routinely?
   - Did people enjoy coping with the crisis?

An examination of this incident will help you see the motivational forces actually at work.

22   Motivation Survey

Purpose

This activity will help you identify how far people really wish to further the purposes of the business.

Process

1. Duplicate the Motivation Survey Questionnaire and ask 20 percent of the people in your organization (or in one department), who are chosen at random, to complete the survey and to return it anonymously to a designated member of management. Tell everyone that the purpose of the questionnaire is to discover what improvements, if any, are needed in the organization, but stress that employees may not see immediate changes as a result of the fact-finding survey.

2. When all the questionnaires have been returned, discuss the results at a management group meeting. Also, do not forget to tell those who were given questionnaires what will result from the data.

MOTIVATION SURVEY QUESTIONNAIRE

Directions. Please complete this questionnaire from your own view-point. Give each statement a score from 1 to 5, as follows:

> 1—never true
> 2—rarely true
> 3—sometimes true
> 4—almost always true
> 5—always true

The maximum score is 75 and the minimum is 15.

Statements	Score
I put as much effort as I can into my job.	_____
I find satisfaction in my work.	_____
I look for opportunities to improve my job.	_____
I want to meet the aims of the organization.	_____
I have no wish to work for a different employer.	_____
My boss creates a really good working atmosphere.	_____
I get sufficient challenge from my job.	_____
I have an important job.	_____
I have responsible work.	_____
I have a "real" job to do.	_____
I have a strong wish to do well.	_____
I set high standards for myself.	_____
In an emergency, I am prepared to work as long as the job demands.	_____
My work produces something I feel proud of.	_____
I do not feel bored at work.	_____
Total	_____

23   Increasing Involvement at Meetings

Purpose

This activity examines whether a more democratic approach to your meetings would be helpful. It can be used at a normally scheduled meeting.

Process

1. Try to forget the usual ground rules for a chairman of a meeting; do not prepare a written agenda.

2. On a flip chart, list those items that you would like to discuss. Ask other participants to expand the list. Then decide jointly on the priority and sequence of each item.

3. If time is at a premium, decide as a group when you will finish the meeting and, if necessary, indicate an approximate time allocation for each item.

4. Proceed with the agenda of the meeting. Allow ten minutes at the end of the session to answer these questions:

   • How did today's meeting compare with previous ones?
   • Have we learned anything that we want to apply next time?

24   Brainstorming

Purpose

This activity is designed to generate creative ideas on any topic as a prelude to change.

Materials

A flip chart and felt-tipped markers are needed.

Process

It is important to follow the rules *exactly*. You will be surprised at the effect of this method if you do.

1. Pick nine top people in your organization and arrange three hours when you can all be together undisturbed (perhaps on a weekend).

2. Select a discussion topic in which change and creativity are important. If a topic does not come easily to mind, use the general topic "ways of improving our business."

3. At the beginning of the meeting, explain that the purpose of the session is to experiment with a technique known as brainstorming, whereby everyone is free to suggest ideas about a specific topic. Emphasize the importance of the rules: (1) all ideas, no matter how absurd or wild, should be contributed; (2) there must be no discussion of an idea—as soon as an idea is introduced, go on to the next one.

4. List the rules on a flip chart and post them as a general reminder for the rest of the session.

5. When everyone understands the rules, begin the brainstorming session with your selected topic or with the one we suggested, which should be written on a flip chart.

6. Brainstorm this topic for at least forty minutes and list (without judgment or discussion) *every* idea suggested.

7. Now divide the participants into two subgroups and ask each group to place each idea into one of these three categories:

    A—important and feasible   B—possible   C—worthless

    Allow one hour for this phase.

8. Ask each group to report on its categorizations by listing its notes on a flip chart, recording all the "A" ideas on one sheet, all the "B" ideas on a second sheet, and all the "C" ideas on a third sheet.

9. Ask each individual to examine the two lists of "A" comments and to choose the two ideas that he feels could make the greatest contribution to improving the business. Note each time an idea is chosen by adding X's or check marks next to the item.

10. Now take the three ideas with the most check marks and ask each subgroup to choose from these the one idea it feels is the most important. Each subgroup then becomes a project team assigned to produce a written plan implementing the idea.

11. After six weeks, the whole group meets to discuss how well plans are progressing and to make any applicable decisions.

12. When these first ideas have been successfully implemented, the subgroups can move on to the others. Project teams can also be rearranged.

25   Yesterday's Good Idea

Purpose

This activity is designed to improve the way in which you, as a group, use creative ideas.

Time Required

Allocate two two-hour sessions, approximately one week apart, for this activity.

Participants

Choose a working group—a top management team or any operating department, including workers, craftsmen, and administrators.

Process

First Session

1. Call a group meeting and tell the participants that the purpose of the session is to discover how well they, as a group, use creative ideas.

2. Ask participants to form pairs by choosing another member of the group with whom they do not work directly. Then ask each pair to take twenty minutes to answer the following question: "What are the best ideas that have been suggested by our group during the last three months?"

3. Each pair reads its list to the entire group and the responses are written on a flip chart.

4. Then each pair considers all the ideas listed and decides which one would be likely to bring the most benefit.

5. After twenty minutes, ask each pair to offer reasons for its choice. The whole group then selects the two ideas with the most promise.

6. In a group discussion, all members are asked to answer the following questions for each of the two ideas selected:

   - Who originated the idea?
   - How was it presented?
   - How was it evaluated?
   - How were plans prepared?
   - Were success criteria established?
   - How was the idea made workable?

- How could more have been derived from this idea?
- What are the general features of the creative work of this group?

These questions should be discussed with the practical experience of the group in mind.

Second Session

1. Ask each participant to evaluate the activity and to share his thoughts with the others. Write comments on a flip chart.

2. Divide the group into three subgroups and give them one hour to consider the following question: "What points would improve the generation and application of creative ideas in the group?"

3. Collect the views of the three subgroups and list them on a flip chart.

4. Finally, ask the group to suggest concrete ways to implement the ideas that were suggested.

26   How Creative Are We?

Purpose

This activity, which is in the form of a check list, is designed to help groups and committees improve the quality of their creative work. If used at the end of a group meeting as a closure session, the activity helps individuals, as well as the whole team, review their performance.

Process

1. At the end of a group meeting, take at least fifteen minutes for members to complete the Creativity Check List.

2. Everyone's views should then be discussed with the group, relevant points defined, and ideas for future improvement collected.

CREATIVITY CHECK LIST

Directions. The purpose of this short questionnaire is to help you think about creativity in your group. In the initial questions, you are to consider *your personal contribution* to the meeting and, later, *your perception of the group as a whole.*

Read the two statements at either end of each line and circle the number that best represents your personal feeling and experience.

Take five or ten minutes to complete the check list and then discuss your views with the group.

Personal Contribution

INVOLVEMENT

| I felt no real involvement at all. | 1 | 2 | 3 | 4 | 5 | 6 | 7 | I felt fully involved with the group throughout the meeting. |

TRUST

| I did not feel free to suggest any new ideas. | 1 | 2 | 3 | 4 | 5 | 6 | 7 | I felt free to suggest anything no matter how unrelated. |

CREATIVITY

| I made no creative contribution. | 1 | 2 | 3 | 4 | 5 | 6 | 7 | I was highly creative. |

USE

| My ideas were not taken seriously. | 1 | 2 | 3 | 4 | 5 | 6 | 7 | My ideas were highly valued. |

Perception of the Whole Group

CREATIVITY

| The group failed to stimulate creativity. | 1 | 2 | 3 | 4 | 5 | 6 | 7 | This is the most creative group I have experienced. |

APPLICATION

| The group almost never used the good ideas suggested. | 1 | 2 | 3 | 4 | 5 | 6 | 7 | Good ideas were very effectively applied. |

ENERGY

| I find this group rather heavy and dull. | 1 | 2 | 3 | 4 | 5 | 6 | 7 | I enjoy being in this energetic group. |

27   Getting to Know You

Purpose

Team development is enhanced when people feel relatively uninhibited toward other members of the group. This activity enables the group to experience what develops when people disclose more personal information than they normally do in such a way as to increase group cohesiveness and identity. It is particularly suitable for commencing a meeting or a workshop; it takes about one hour to complete.

Participants

This activity is best suited for new groups or for those who wish to work together more fully. Only those participants who volunteer should participate in the activity; there should be no pressure to make people take part.

Process

1. When the group convenes, explain the purpose of the activity. Emphasize that only those who wish to participate should do so.

2. Ask each participant to select a partner he knows least well.

3. Distribute a copy of the Getting to Know You Questionnaire to each person and explain that the activity involves one person interviewing the other by asking the questions on the questionnaire. Let each pair decide who will be the first interviewer; he should ask only those questions he would be prepared to answer himself. The respondent replies only if he wishes and in as much detail as he desires.

4. When the sequence of questions is finished by one interviewer, partners change roles, and the same procedure is repeated.

5. At the end of the questioning, the partners discuss their reactions to the activity. Then the entire group can examine what it learned from the experience.

GETTING TO KNOW YOU QUESTIONNAIRE

Directions:

1. Ask only those questions that you are also prepared to answer.
2. Ask the questions in sequence.
3. You are free to decline to answer if you wish.
4. When you have completed the questioning, discuss your feelings.

QUESTIONS

1. How do you feel now?
2. Do you like telling others about yourself?
3. What do you think about black and white people marrying?
4. Do you feel that your own feelings are important?
5. Are you religious?
6. Do you enjoy work?
7. What do you dislike most?
8. What is your most basic belief?
9. What bores you most?
10. When do you feel at your best?
11. Do your relationships with women (men) satisfy you?
12. Are you able to meet your needs in life?
13. If you had one magic wish and could do one thing, what would it be?
14. How do you feel now?
15. How do you feel about me?

28   Microlab

Purpose

This activity is designed to help people become more open and friendly by breaking through some of the conventional barriers to communication, a technique borrowed from encounter groups.

Some people may feel that this activity explores personal feelings too deeply, by demanding physical as well as vocal exchange; however, we have found it a powerful tool in demonstrating the importance of how people feel toward each other. Participation should always be entirely voluntary and participants must realize that the activity requires a modicum of risk.

Time Required

The activity takes about one and one-half hours to complete. Because it is important to keep to the time schedule, one participant should function as timekeeper.

Participants

Between four and twelve participants are optimal.

Setting Required

The room needs to be large enough to accommodate the movement of the group. Sufficient chairs are placed in a circle.

Process

1. When participants are seated, describe the purpose of the Micro-lab activity and discuss the following ground rules:

   • Express your feelings but avoid theoretical discussion.
   • View the microlab as an experiment and suspend judgment.
   • Watch what happens inside of you as the activity proceeds.
   • Be responsible for yourself; do only those things that you wish to.
   • Be as honest as you can, but always try to be helpful rather than negative.

   Everyone should have a chance to ask questions or to offer comments.

2. The participants' first task is to describe how they are feeling *now*. Ask each person to describe his own feelings—is he nervous, excited, confused, bored? No more than two minutes should be allocated to each person.

3. Participants stand in a circle. One at a time, each person enters the circle, faces the other members of the group, and tells each participant in turn what he feels about that person at that moment. He should simply state his feelings, not make judgments.

4. To illustrate the influential and powerful nature of groups, the following exercise is conducted.

   Clear the chairs away and make sure that there are no obstacles. The participants form a circle around one member, link arms, and face outward. The member imprisoned in the center must try to get out of the circle, while those making up the circle try in a fair manner to prevent this. Each person has a turn being in the center and experiencing the feelings of being imprisoned and trying to break out.

5. The entire group discusses the experience for ten minutes.

6. Next, each person finds a partner. One member of each pair closes his eyes while the other partner leads him around the room by very light pressure on his shoulders. After three minutes of this, partners reverse roles. At all times, partners must keep moving about the room, experiencing how it feels to be dependent on another person.

7. Seated again as a group, participants discuss their feelings about the activity without intellectualizing. They should consider whether their feelings about other members of the group have changed.

8. Finally, each group member sits in silence for three minutes, attempting to feel as physically relaxed as possible and to be sensitive to each sound or movement. Then each person tells the group something that he wishes to say to the others. Everyone who wishes to speak does so; there is no hurry. Long speeches, however, should be discouraged. When each person has had a chance to speak, the microlab closes.

29 Organizational Mirroring

Purpose

All of us form views of other groups of people. Sometimes these views are accurate, but often they act as a barrier to working together effectively. Often we are better off when we know about the judgments we make about others and also about their views of us.

This activity helps us to see ourselves as others see us.

Time Required

One-half day.

Participants

Two separate groups are needed for this activity. The process has been used successfully with such groups as top and middle managers, sales and production people, supervisors and operatives, teachers and students, nurses and patients, and blacks and whites.

Process

1. Introduce the activity to both groups with a short explanation of its goals and procedure. Then separate the two groups and ask each to prepare a list of twenty-five adjectives that best describe the other group. Choose a spokesman for each group to record the list of adjectives on a flip chart.

2. In approximately one hour, both groups reunite and the spokesmen read and display their lists. Each leader summarizes his group's position by drawing attention to the key words. All participants then consider the two lists silently for two minutes.

3. Participants divide into subgroups of four members each, two people from each working group. Each subgroup takes approximately one hour to discuss how people see each other. In the last ten minutes, each person writes on a sheet of paper what he or she has learned from the exchange of views. These sheets, which remain anonymous, are collected and shared by the entire group.

4. Following this discussion, the leader should try to get either a commitment to take some beneficial action or an agreement to meet again.

30   Process Review

Purpose

This activity is designed to study meetings for the purpose of improving team functioning.

Process

1. For the maximum effect of the activity, choose an important meeting that you attend regularly. It is, however, also possible to choose any meeting. If the group is prepared to carry out a self-study of its meetings with the aim of improving effectiveness, appoint one member to become an observer for one or two meetings.

2. The observer can introduce his role to the group by making the following points:

   "My role is to observe and record what I see occurring. At the end of the session, I will report my observations to you so that we can all review how we behave in real situations.

   "The aim of this method is to help us gain insight and awareness into ourselves and into the processes of a working group. Hopefully, this will give us more control over how we respond in all situations.

   "During the sessions, I will be particularly considering the following points:

   - Is the purpose of the group clearly understood by everyone?
   - Is good use being made of the time available?
   - Are personal aims conflicting with the group's aims?
   - Is the group avoiding issues that may be difficult or unpleasant?
   - Do people really listen to others?
   - Does discussion deal with facts and verifiable information, or does it deal with speculation and opinion?

   "Since being an observer does not entitle me to any superior vision, I may see things incorrectly. I hope, however, that this activity will help us improve our teamwork."

3. The observer, who takes no part in the discussions of the meetings, watches carefully what occurs.

4. The observer's review at the end of the meeting takes approximately one-half hour. Initially, he should use the Process Review Check List as a guide. He should try to be as helpful as possible by describing, rather than interpreting, what he actually saw.

PROCESS REVIEW CHECK LIST

Who contributed most?

Who contributed least?

How clear was the purpose of the discussion?

How well did people listen to each other?

Were creative ideas suggested?

Did the meeting serve to bridge different interests?

What were the most helpful actions?

Was the time well used?

Were difficult issues dealt with thoroughly?

Was discussion factual whenever possible?

31   Group Climate

Purpose

This activity is designed to provide some information about how group members view their particular group or team.

Participants

The activity is most useful for a group that works together and wishes to improve its performance.

Process

1. If an intact work group wishes to learn more about its group climate, ask each person to fill out the Group Climate Questionnaire anonymously and to return it to a designated person, who will collect the various scores and calculate averages for the actual situation and for the desired situation.

2. When the information is charted and averaged, arrange a one-hour meeting to enable the group to discuss the implications of the data.

3. The group should then decide whether concrete steps need to be taken to improve the group climate.

GROUP CLIMATE QUESTIONNAIRE

Directions. Circle the number from 1 to 10 that you think best represents the group's present situation. Also put the letter "D" over the number that represents the group's situation as you would like it to be. This will enable you to compare the actual with the desired situation.

Standards

Does the group set high-quality standards for itself in respect to its principles and practice? Does it think broadly and deeply into the wider consequences of its work? Does it take care with its work?

Standards are very low in our group.	1	2	3	4	5	6	7	8	9	10	Our group sets high standards.

Responsibility

Are group members given the opportunity to exercise the responsibilities formally given to them? Do people feel a sense of personal responsibility for the effectiveness of the group?

Responsibility is not given to or accepted by the individual.	1	2	3	4	5	6	7	8	9	10	There is great emphasis on personal responsibility within our group.

Conformity

Does the group have rules, procedures, policies, and traditions that are difficult to escape? Are the ideas of the senior staff considered law?

Our group conforms rigidly to a set pattern.	1	2	3	4	5	6	7	8	9	10	Our group is open and conformity is not a problem.

Benefits

Do group members feel appreciated and rewarded by membership in the group, or are relationships characterized by criticism, insults, and retribution?

Group members feel unappreciated.	1	2	3	4	5	6	7	8	9	10	Group members feel rewarded and benefited.

Effectiveness

Is the group well organized and does it work clearly and methodically toward objectives?

Our group is chaotic and confused.	1	2	3	4	5	6	7	8	9	10	Our group is clear and effective.

Leadership

Does the leadership of the group help members contribute fully and effectively? Does leadership change according to the task undertaken? Is leadership based on outstanding merit?

Our group is dominated by ineffective leaders.	1	2	3	4	5	6	7	8	9	10	Our group is competently led by those who are best qualified.

32   Which New Car?

Purpose

This activity enables groups to learn about the effect of personal aims on collective decisions. It can also be used to help a team develop its effectiveness.

Participants

Four to eight participants are needed. If there are more than eight, form another group. It is helpful if one participant acts as an observer, whose role is to help the group learn from the experience. The observer, who takes no part in the role play, should be selected before the session. (Follow the instructions in activity 30, "Process Review.")

Materials

The Which New Car? Role Sheet should be duplicated and each role placed in a separate envelope.

Process

1. Explain that the task of the group is to choose a new type of company car to replace the Excell, which is being discontinued. Only one make of car can be purchased for the organization. The three types available are:

   The Speedster—a small but rather fast and comfortable sports car.

   The Villager—a larger vehicle, suitable for carrying five adults and a good deal of luggage. However, the Villager looks old-fashioned and is rather sluggish. It is considered a safe, dependable vehicle.

   The Traveller—a reasonably fast, modern-looking vehicle that has sufficient room for a family. However, a recent impartial report suggests that the Traveller has a worse accident record than the Villager.

2. Distribute the roles randomly to group members. Participants should see only their own roles, which they must follow.

3. The group discusses the problem for twenty minutes.

4. After the role play, the group reviews the process to gain insight into team functioning.

5. If there was an observer, he gives his report of the experience. A group discussion of individual reactions follows.

6. The final stage is to discuss whether the insights learned can be applied in the day-to-day working situation.

WHICH NEW CAR? ROLE SHEET

Role 1

You have a large family and want a full-sized, versatile vehicle. The Villager is the only vehicle you want.

Role 2

You want a vehicle that has high prestige and that makes a good impression on your customers.

Role 3

You feel that the safety problems are overrated and that the Traveller is the best buy. Also, your neighbor is delighted with his Traveller.

Role 4

You have no fixed opinions about a vehicle and will support the strongest case.

Role 5

From your point of view, comfort is the most important factor. You have two small children.

Role 6

You disapprove of the consultative process in deciding this matter and feel that the company ought to make a decision solely on financial grounds. You want management to decide on the basis of an impartial study of purchase and operating costs.

Role 7

You wish to show your ability to act as an impartial chairman. However, you do have three teenage children.

----

33   A Question of Principle

Purpose

The activity is designed to examine the principles underlying major decisions.

Time Required

Two short sessions, approximately two weeks apart, are necessary.

Participants

It is best to involve the entire senior group of the organization. The ideal number of participants is ten.

Process

Session One

1. Explain the purpose of the activity to the senior group members.

2. Divide the group into three subgroups and ask each to choose the two major decisions of the past year that most affected people in the organization. Allow thirty minutes for the subgroups to discuss the options and then collect all views.

3. The entire group selects the three decisions that seem most significant and again breaks into subgroups to review the decisions and to select the most significant one using the Key Decisions Check List. Each subgroup can meet as needed during the next week as it undertakes the required research.

Session Two

1. Each subgroup has fifteen minutes to report on its investigation, and then the whole group discusses the selections.

2. A final stage is spent discussing the practical steps that can be taken to increase the quality of the organization's decision making.

KEY DECISIONS CHECK LIST

1. Who made the decision?

2. Who was consulted?

3. Were the human implications systematically considered?

4. What was the effect of the decision?

5. Were the actual effects foreseen?

6. What assumptions about people underlay the decision?

7. What is the effect on "the quality of working life"?

8. What is the effect on the community at large?

9. What is the effect on the environment?

10. What principles did the manner of decision making demonstrate to those involved?

34 Theory "X" and Theory "Y"

Purpose

Organizations, like communities, develop traditions, customs, and habits that give them a particular flavor or culture. Because the management is likely to enforce the traditions and customs of an organization, it is often worth questioning whether they are realistic and relevant in today's world.

This activity helps reveal the prevailing attitudes that determine the organizational climate. Once brought into the open, these attitudes can be dealt with more effectively.

Process

1. Ask a group of people to complete the Theory "X"—Theory "Y" Questionnaire. It is best to start with a management team and then proceed to other intact work groups.

2. Ask that the questionnaires be returned anonymously to a particular person by a certain date. The selected person then analyzes the questionnaires and produces a chart showing the average management style actually prevailing at the moment—A—and the average preferred management style—B.

3. After the chart has been prepared, call a meeting of those who completed the questionnaire.

    Explain the aim of the meeting, display the chart, and discuss the management style prevailing within the organization. Identify the concrete steps that could improve management practice in the light of these findings. (Allow at least one and one-half hours for this phase.)

THEORY "X"—THEORY "Y" QUESTIONNAIRE

Directions. This questionnaire is intended to identify the present management style in your organization and your preferred management style.

Read each question and place the letter "A" over the numeral that best reflects management's *present* attitude toward the people who work for the organization.

Then consider what you feel management's attitude *should* be and indicate this with the letter "B."

A—management's present attitude

B—what you would prefer management's attitude to be

The average person inherently dislikes work.	1	2	3	4	5	6	7	8	9	10	Work is as natural as rest to people.
People must be directed to work.	1	2	3	4	5	6	7	8	9	10	People will exercise self-discretion and self-control.
People wish to avoid responsibility.	1	2	3	4	5	6	7	8	9	10	People enjoy real responsibility.
People feel that achievement in work is irrelevant.	1	2	3	4	5	6	7	8	9	10	Achievement is highly valued by people.
Most people are dull and uncreative.	1	2	3	4	5	6	7	8	9	10	Most people have great potential, imagination, and creativity.
Money is the only real reason for working.	1	2	3	4	5	6	7	8	9	10	Money is only part of the benefits of work.

People lack the desire to improve their own quality of life.	1	2	3	4	5	6	7	8	9	10	People have real needs to improve the quality of life.

Having an objective is a form of imprisonment.	1	2	3	4	5	6	7	8	9	10	Objectives are welcomed as an aid to effectiveness.

35   Principles Game*

Purpose

The activity is designed to show how principles emerge in competition and to emphasize the merits of collaboration.

Participants

An optimal choice is an intact work group or two groups (of not more than eight members each) that sometimes work together.

Process

1. Divide the group into two subgroups—a "green" team and a "red" team. Seat the groups apart from each other and ask each team not to interact with the other during the meetings except when instructed to do so.

2. Distribute a copy of the Principles Game Tally Sheet to each participant. Give members time to study the directions and scoring and ask if there are any questions. Tell the two teams that the objective is for each group to score as many points as possible. Explain that no one will probably understand clearly how the game is played until the activity proceeds.

3. Round 1 begins. Each team is given five minutes to decide on a letter. When the time is up, each team announces its decision and the scoring is computed on the Principles Game Tally Sheet.

4. Rounds 2 and 3 are conducted in the same manner as Round 1, but with three minutes for discussion in each round.

5. For Round 4, both teams send one representative to a neutral place to negotiate for three minutes. Then the representatives return to confer with their teams. After three minutes, each team announces its decision and the outcome of the round is doubled.

6. Rounds 5 through 8 proceed in the same manner as the first three rounds, with three minutes for discussion in each.

7. In Round 9, another special round conducted like Round 4, the outcome is multiplied by 5.

---

*This activity is adapted from "Prisoner's Dilemma: An Intergroup Competition," in J. W. Pfeiffer & J. E. Jones (Eds.), *A Handbook of Structured Experiences for Human Relations Training*, Volume III. La Jolla, Ca.: University Associates, 1971 & 1974.

8. Round 10 is conducted in the same way as Round 9, except that the results are multiplied by 10.

9. The entire group meets to tally the final scores and to discuss who won and why. The following questions should be considered:

How did you feel about the other team as the game progressed?
How did you feel about other members of your own team?
How could you have achieved a higher score?
What lessons are there for management?

PRINCIPLES GAME TALLY SHEET

Directions. For ten rounds, the green team will choose either an *A* or a *B* and the red team will choose either an *X* or a *Y*. The score for each team is determined by both teams' joint decision. It is computed according to the following schedule.

AX—Both teams win 3 points.

AY—Green team loses 6 points;
 Red team wins 6 points.

BX—Green team wins 6 points;
 Red team loses 6 points.

BY—Both teams lose 3 points.

Round	Choice		Cumulative points	
	Green Team	Red Team	Green Team	Red Team
1				
2				
3				
*4				
5				
6				
7				
8				
**9				
***10				

*Results are doubled for this round.
**Results are multiplied by 5 for this round.
***Results are multiplied by 10 for this round.

36   Are We Running a Kindergarten?

Purpose

This activity is designed to examine whether the organization considers and treats people as irresponsible children or as responsible adults.

Participants

This activity is useful for a group that actually works together regularly.

Time and Setting Required

Two hours in an undisturbed setting are needed.

Process

1. At the start of the session, distribute copies of the Are We Running a Kindergarten? Questionnaire and ask each participant to answer the questions by choosing either option (a) or option (b), whichever most closely corresponds to his personal experience in the organization.

2. When the questionnaires are completed, each person announces his choices, which are averaged for the whole group.

3. Then the group discusses the outcomes based on the following questions:

   Why do we disagree on certain questions?
   Is our predominant style to treat people as adults (a) or as children (b)?
   How can we treat people more as adults?
   What concrete steps can we take in the next month to improve the situation?

ARE WE RUNNING A KINDERGARTEN? QUESTIONNAIRE

1. ☐ (a) We treat people as independent beings here.

   ☐ (b) Our people are largely dependent on management.

2. ☐ (a) We treat people as if they really make a significant contribution to the organization and to society.

   ☐ (b) Our people are not thought capable of making a significant contribution to the company or to society.

3. ☐ (a) We consider people quite responsible; therefore, we give them responsibility.

   ☐ (b) Our system does not, in practice, give most people real responsibility.

4. ☐ (a) We generally believe that people can give care and attention to their jobs without control.

   ☐ (b) Our system is based on the assumption that people are generally careless and incapable of sustained attention.

5. ☐ (a) We give people credit for being able to take a broad-minded view and to make sound judgments.

   ☐ (b) We normally expect most people to be narrow minded and not able to make sound judgments.

6. ☐ (a) We believe that people are fundamentally energetic and capable of getting things done.

   ☐ (b) We assume that our people will avoid work if they get half a chance.

37   Succession Planning

Purpose

Planning for succession is necessary because organizations can survive almost indefinitely, whereas people grow old and eventually retire. Everyone in the organization must eventually be replaced, and, although it is often difficult to think about, it is of critical importance to see where tomorrow's people will come from.

    This activity will enable you to examine whether there are problems associated with staffing your organization in the future.

Process

1. Reproduce the Succession Planning Sheet or make one of your own.

2. In the first column, make a list of all managers' and supervisors' job titles and the names of the current jobholders.

3. Then list all other key jobs (and employees' names) that either take more than three months to learn properly or for which it would be a real nuisance to replace the present jobholder.

4. Check the columns on the sheet that best represent the amount of time each employee will likely remain at that job. Also fill in the last column—the person most likely to succeed—for each job.

5. Finally, list all the jobs that you expect to create in the future.

    If the same names appear several times in the last column, you should begin to get worried. If there are more blanks than you are happy with, the implications for each case need to be considered separately.

    After reviewing the results of the Succession Planning Sheet, you may find that your problems can be solved by some careful planning and training. If the problems really seem massive, however, you may need some good advice in the matter. The greater the gap between the company's future needs and your available people resources, the more serious is the problem.

SUCCESSION PLANNING SHEET

Job Name	Is employee likely to be here in:					Name of Person Most Likely to Succeed
	One Year	Two Years	Three Years	Five Years	Ten Years	
Managers/ Supervisors						
Other key jobs						
Possible new jobs						

38   Individual Management-Development Requirements

Purpose

If managers are to feel responsible for their own learning, they need to establish their own development needs and to take steps to increase their competence. This activity is designed to help each manager determine how best to do this.

Process

Each individual manager fills out a copy of the Manager Development-Requirements Sheet and discusses it with his or her boss. Many managers also find it helpful to talk things over with a colleague, friend, wife, husband, or outside specialist in management training.

MANAGER DEVELOPMENT-REQUIREMENTS SHEET

1. Name _____

2. Function/Position _____

3. What are the main activities that you perform?

4. What changes in each of these activities do you expect in the next year?

5. What aspects of your job present the most difficulty? Give examples.

6. What do you need to help you learn to:

   (a) cope with changes in your job?

   (b) deal with the difficulties you face?

   (c) help your general development?

7. Which of these training methods would be most relevant to you? (Indicate order of priority by ranking from 1 to 11—1 being most relevant.)

☐ 1. Management education course at a business school.

☐ 2. Short job-related courses/seminars.

☐ 3. Visits to other companies, etc.

☐ 4. Reading.

☐ 5. Internal courses.

☐ 6. Coaching by your manager.

☐ 7. Coaching by others.

☐ 8. Discussion groups with colleagues.

☐ 9. Projects.

☐ 10. Transfer to another section or function.

☐ 11. Short course in human relations management.

8. Make a specific proposal to meet your development needs, establishing your own objectives and preferred method of learning. (See activity 41, "Establishing an Objective.")

39 Values of the Present Management-Development System

Purpose

All organizations develop people in some way. Often big organizations have carefully planned procedures to accomplish management development. This activity is designed to reveal the basic principles and values that underlie your present approach to management development, whether it be completely informal or highly systematic.

Process

1. If your organization is small, invite everyone with a staff or management job to complete a copy of the Management-Development Questionnaire. If you have a larger organization, a 20 percent sample should be sufficient. Ask that the questionnaires be returned to a particular person on a specific day.

2. Call a meeting of about six people in your firm who feel most strongly about management development, call them the "M.D. review group," and present them with the average scores on the questionnaire.

3. After absorbing that data, the group's assignment is to produce a brief written statement, answering these three questions:

   - What principles *should* underlie our management-development practice?

   - According to the survey, what principles *actually* underlie our management-development practice?

   - What needs to be done, if anything, to better match reality and aim?

MANAGEMENT-DEVELOPMENT QUESTIONNAIRE

Directions. Please fill out this questionnaire from your own practical experience in your organization. The results will be used to review how well current practices meet the needs of the situation.

Mark the letter *A* over the numeral that you feel best represents the current situation in the organization. Also put the letter *D* over the numeral that best represents the situation in which you would like to see the organization in the future.

    A represents the *actual* situation as you see it.

    D represents your view of the *desirable* situation.

Your scores are anonymous and will be averaged. You will also be told about the results of this survey.

1. The company's management-development policy is perfectly clear to me.   1   2   3   4   5   6   7   The company's management-development policy is unclear to me.

2. Management development is taken seriously here.   1   2   3   4   5   6   7   Management development is an empty phrase here.

3. Management development has helped me greatly in the past.   1   2   3   4   5   6   7   Management development has not helped me at all.

4. The management-development systems here are appropriate and helpful.   1   2   3   4   5   6   7   The management-development systems obscure real needs.

5. Management development is sufficiently organized and controlled.   1   2   3   4   5   6   7   Management development is unbusinesslike and disorganized.

6. Management development helps managers grow stronger.   1   2   3   4   5   6   7   Management development does not help personal growth.

7. Managers find it easy to acquire the skills they need.　　1　2　3　4　5　6　7　Managers find it difficult to acquire opportunities for training.

8. Managers are helped to be creative and innovative.　　1　2　3　4　5　6　7　Managers are creative and innovative at their peril.

9. I have help in clarifying my own needs.　　1　2　3　4　5　6　7　No one helps me clarify my own needs.

10. Management-development practices make a good contribution to the organization.　　1　2　3　4　5　6　7　Management-development practices contribute nothing to the organization's effectiveness.

40 How and Why?

Purpose

The activity is designed to examine the real reasons for organizational practices and then to focus on the action required.

Process

Think about a current practice in your organization or a suggestion and ask yourself *why* you want to pursue it. Continue asking "Why?" to each answer until you arrive at the real objective.

Then consider your last answer and ask *how* you will reach the objective. Continue asking yourself "How?" until you have a clearer plan of action.

For example, asking *why* a new person is needed could bring the answer "in order to perform the task." Asking "Why?" again could reveal that the task is really unnecessary.

If, however, your response indicates that the task is necessary, asking the question "How?" could lead to a solution other than recruitment.

This simple procedure often helps to identify *real* as opposed to *stated* objectives. Asking "Why?" opens up issues and helps lead to meaningful discussion. It also helps clarify what needs to be done as opposed to what one assumes needs to be done. Asking "How?" limits issues and facilitates the move toward a plan of action.

41   Establishing an Objective

Purpose

This activity enables you to explore a different way of delegating a task.

Process

1. Decide on a task (or tasks) that you want completed by one of your subordinates.

2. Meet with him and discuss the task in terms of the *output* that is needed rather than the *action* required to achieve the completion of the task (such as, to achieve so much production rather than to manage the department efficiently).

3. Set a time for the completion of the task and discuss what measurements will be used to assess whether the task has been completed satisfactorily. Also agree on a date for a review and at that meeting consider whether this simple procedure helped either of you.

42   Exploring Understandings of a Job

Purpose

This activity is designed to help managers and subordinates discover how well they share a common understanding of the purpose and function of a particular job.

Process

1. Ask a manager to write down what he expects from one of his colleagues or subordinates over the next six months and the data or evidence to be used to judge performance.

   This is not simply a formal management-by-objectives approach, because it deals with feelings as well as facts. A good way for the manager to begin his statement of expectations is with the following words: "I expect that you will . . ."

   For example, a typical statement would be "I expect that you will produce a quarterly report that suggests concrete methods to improve our systems. I will judge this as being successful if, as a result of your suggestions, we achieve a savings in cost or an improvement in our service."

2. Independently, the colleague or subordinate produces a list of his own expectations in relation to himself and his boss, and makes a request for the support and resources he needs. Here the form of words is "I expect that I will . . ."

3. Both people meet to share their expectations and requirements.

   It is necessary for each person to understand the other's point of view and to see what is significant to him or her. Then there needs to be a form of bargaining such as the following:

   "If I am expected to do this, then I will need these resources."

   "I will give this much time toward this aim."

   "We really need to check this out before we can go forward."

   "Can this realistically be accomplished?"

   "Yes, I feel committed to this point."

4. Both people work on the problems until they are resolved. A number of sessions may be needed.

43   Long-Range Planning

Purpose

A long-range plan can be an invaluable operating guide or a largely irrelevant piece of fiction. This activity will enable you to see how well your present long-range planning procedures fulfill your managers' expectations.

Process

1. Duplicate the Long-Range Planning Questionnaire and send a copy to each manager in the organization who is directly affected by the long-range plan.

2. When the questionnaires are returned, determine the average score by giving five points for an "A" answer, four for a "B," three for a "C," two for a "D," and one for an "E."

3. If the total average is below twenty-five points, which suggests poor long-range planning, form a high-powered project group to investigate the planning process.

LONG-RANGE PLANNING QUESTIONNAIRE

The purpose of this questionnaire is to discover how well the present long-term plan is meeting the needs of managers. The results may call for further investigation into the planning process.

Directions. Check the box that is nearest to your present experience.

1. I feel that there is full top-management support for the long-term plan.

A ☐	B ☐	C ☐	D ☐	E ☐
Strongly agree	Agree	Moderately agree	Disagree	Strongly disagree

2. Top management clearly makes decisions on the basis of the plan.

A ☐	B ☐	C ☐	D ☐	E ☐
Strongly agree	Agree	Moderately agree	Disagree	Strongly disagree

3. Proper resources are allocated for planning.

A ☐	B ☐	C ☐	D ☐	E ☐
Strongly agree	Agree	Moderately agree	Disagree	Strongly disagree

4. The plan makes good sense to me, personally.

A ☐	B ☐	C ☐	D ☐	E ☐
Strongly agree	Agree	Moderately agree	Disagree	Strongly disagree

5. Good short-term plans evolve from the long-term plan.

A ☐	B ☐	C ☐	D ☐	E ☐
Strongly agree	Agree	Moderately agree	Disagree	Strongly disagree

6. I feel that those responsible for long-term planning are capable and well qualified.

A ☐	B ☐	C ☐	D ☐	E ☐
Strongly agree	Agree	Moderately agree	Disagree	Strongly disagree

7. The organization is ready to change things substantially if necessary.

A ☐   B ☐   C ☐   D ☐   E ☐
Strongly   Agree   Moderately   Disagree   Strongly
agree   agree   disagree

8. I feel a part of the planning process.

A ☐   B ☐   C ☐   D ☐   E ☐
Strongly   Agree   Moderately   Disagree   Strongly
agree   agree   disagree

44   Meeting Objectives

Purpose

Research has shown that organizations that have a clear understanding of where they are going are more likely to be successful. This activity is designed to help you gain that clear understanding.

Time Required

A whole day is best for this activity.

Participants

The activity can be conducted with a team of people who normally work together or it can be used as a planning session with directors. The approach works particularly well with smaller organizations or with departments of larger organizations.

Process

Set up a team meeting. Ask one member of the group to come prepared to give a short talk (about twenty minutes) on setting objectives as a methodical way of doing business.

First Session

1. Explain the purpose of the activity and invite the member chosen as speaker to deliver his introductory speech.

2. Ask each member of the group to take twenty minutes to list the organization's main objectives on a sheet of paper.

3. Collect these sheets and display each member's points on a flip chart. Then have the group identify which objectives are real priorities and list these separately. (At least one hour should be allocated for this phase.)

4. In groups or individually, assess the firm's resources, provisionally allocate them to meet the objectives, and identify what needs to be done to develop the people involved.

Second Session

1. Begin the second half of the session by checking whether the objectives are still valid or if they need revision or amendment.

2. Ask each person individually (or in pairs) to take one or more of the objectives and to prepare a forward plan that will lead to the achievement of the objectives. (Approximately one hour should be devoted to this phase.)

3. Invite each person to discuss his plan and to suggest action steps to the group.

4. Draw the following diagram on a flip chart.

5. Then, discuss these two questions:
   - How well does this summarize an effective way of working for us?
   - What can we do to use what we have learned?

45   The Empty Chair*

Purpose

This activity is designed to help people find ways of dealing with intractable problems.

    Because this activity is slightly more advanced than some of the others, it is best to have some prior experience in conducting a few of the other activities. Although the process may seem strange and complicated to participants at first, the method works well and is often very revealing.

Materials

Each pair of participants needs an extra, empty chair.

Process

1. Thoroughly describe all the steps involved in the activity and ask the group to divide into pairs. Each pair should find some privacy and be seated, with an empty chair nearby.

2. One member of each pair begins by describing to his partner a problem that he finds difficult or impossible to handle. The other member of the pair listens to the problem and then helps his partner identify the two main sides of the dilemma.

3. The person with the problem is to carry on a dialog between both sides of the problem, while the other member acts as an observer. The first partner begins by talking to the empty chair from the viewpoint of the first side of his dilemma. Then he moves to the empty chair and takes the viewpoint of the second side of the problem. The dialog continues until each side of the problem has been fully explored.

4. In the next step, the observer asks his partner to sit in his (the observer's) chair and to take an impartial view of the problem, by suggesting possible remedies and solutions to the empty chair (representing himself).

5. When this step is completed, the observer describes the situation as he sees it. Then the pair switches roles, giving the observer a chance to work through his own problem.

---

    *This activity is adapted from "Empty Chair: An Extended Group Design," in J. W. Pfeiffer & J. E. Jones (Eds.), *A Handbook of Structured Experiences for Human Relations Training*, Volume III. La Jolla, Ca.: University Associates, 1971 & 1974.

46   Rob Peter to Pay Paul

Purpose

This activity enables a group to explore how people value different occupations. It is especially useful for negotiating committees.

Time Required

One hour is needed.

Process

1. Give each member of the group fifteen minutes to fill out a copy of the Rob Peter to Pay Paul Sheet. Then list all the scores on a flip chart and calculate a group average.

2. Each person should then discuss the reasons underlying his choices. During this stage, deviations from the group norm can be discussed. The discussions can take place either in small subgroups or in the entire group.

ROB PETER TO PAY PAUL SHEET

Directions. Consider the list of occupations below and rank them in order of the importance you feel they have. Write the number "1" for the occupation you feel is most important, the number "2" for the next important, and so on.

Decide your own criteria for what is important and define it at the end of the sheet.

Although it may be difficult for you to make a decision without more information, please make a choice in each case.

Ranking   Occupation

_____   A. Air pilot (civil)

_____   B. Taxi driver

_____   C. Typist

_____   D. Craftsman electrician

_____   E. Doctor (medical)

_____   F. Supervisor

_____   G. University lecturer

_____   H. Union official (local, full-time)

_____   I. Plant manager (500 employees)

_____   J. Training manager

_____   K. Process operative

_____   L. Butcher

_____   M. Accountant

_____   N. Computer operator

_____   O. Fork-lift truck driver

————   P. Coal miner (face worker)

————   Q. Elevator operator

————   R. Bank manager

————   S. Television news announcer

————   T. Housewife

My definition of "important" is:

47   Roadbuilding to Equity

Purpose

This activity is designed to evaluate your present organizational mechanisms for dealing with benefits, rewards, and punishments.

Participants

The activity is usually undertaken by managers, but it is also especially helpful for mixed groups, including hourly employees. A minimum of six people is required, with a maximum of sixteen.

Time Required

Two and one-half hours are required.

Process

1. Introduce the activity to the group and distribute paper and a pencil to each participant.

2. Then divide the group into two approximately equal subgroups and separate each group to allow for privacy.

3. Distribute the appropriate Subgroup Sheet to each participant and tell each group that it has forty-five minutes to complete the task.

4. At the end of this period, the whole group reassembles for fifteen minutes to discuss each subgroup's conclusions and to ask questions.

5. A copy of the Roadbuilding to Equity Questionnaire is distributed to each participant. When the questionnaires are completed, each person calculates his own score and the scores are announced and then averaged.

   A score of 22 to 28 points indicates that the employees believe the system is a good one. A score of 18 to 21 points means that the organization should consider updating its present system. A score of 12 to 17 points means that a radical change in the fundamental policy is needed. Below 12 points indicates that your policy is very inadequate.

6. The final stage is to discuss the situation with the aim of identifying three clear action steps to tackle the problem.

SUBGROUP 1 SHEET

Directions. Prepare a brief statement of the organization's policy in relation to benefits as you see it. Then list the present mechanisms used for consultation and decision making in relation to rewards and punishments.

SUBGROUP 2 SHEET

Directions. Prepare a list of issues relating to benefits, rewards, and punishments that you feel need to be discussed in the organization.

ROADBUILDING TO EQUITY QUESTIONNAIRE

I believe that our present benefits policy and procedures:

									Points
are totally inadequate;	1	2	3	4	5	6	7	cannot be improved.	☐
are unclear and confused;	1	2	3	4	5	6	7	are clear and logical.	☐
are unjustly applied;	1	2	3	4	5	6	7	are well-balanced.	☐
are a millstone around our necks;	1	2	3	4	5	6	7	will meet our future needs well.	☐
								Total	☐

48   Us or Them

Purpose

This activity, which takes the form of a debate, is designed to clarify differences between the needs of individuals and the needs of the organization.

Time Required

Two hours.

Process

1. Divide the group into two subgroups and brief each one separately.

2. In the first subgroup, each member is to describe what benefits he or she would like to gain from working in the organization over the next five years. (Allow approximately ten minutes for this.) One member of the group is appointed spokesman. The spokesman's assignment is to listen to all persons' lists of desired benefits and then to develop a representative picture of the subgroup as a whole. (Twenty minutes.) The spokesman will later be asked to make a ten-minute speech presenting the case for these needs.

3. The second subgroup's task is to describe as realistically and accurately as possible the probable benefits that the organization will offer to employees over the next five years. (Thirty minutes.) One member is chosen to be the subgroup's chief debater; his task is to explain the company's position and to defend it if attacked.

4. When both groups have organized their cases, the debate begins. The chief debater from the second subgroup describes what benefits employees can realistically expect from the organization over the next five years. (Ten minutes.) This is followed by a speech from the spokesman of the first subgroup describing the employees' needs over the next five years. (Ten minutes.)

5. Following the two speeches, participants may bring up any remaining points and arguments. Then participants vote on whether they believe that the company's benefits scheme will meet their needs over the next five years.

49   How Does Our Pay Compare?

Purpose

The activity is designed to examine whether wage rates in your organization are competitive.

Process

1. Assign someone, preferably a person with enough initiative to do some detective work, the project of gathering as much information as possible about comparable wages in other organizations.

2. Make a special point of asking new recruits and those who leave about wage rates at their last or new place of work.

3. Then set up a meeting to compare your organization's wage rates with those you have collected. Make sure the meeting includes those managers who have difficulty recruiting workers. Discuss whether there would be any value in making this a regular exercise.

50   Who Makes the Decisions About Pay?

Purpose

This activity is designed to examine who takes the initiative about pay.

Participants

The activity can be undertaken by a group of managers, by a group of employee representatives, by a mixture of these two groups, or simply by an individual.

Process

1. On a sheet of paper, list the last ten changes in the pay of individual employees in the organization.

2. Then list the last ten changes in the pay of groups of employees (or departments).

3. Ask how these changes occurred, i.e., was the initiative taken by management, unions, individuals, or whom?

4. Try to determine if it would have been better had the initiative come from a different source and if there is any action that could facilitate a better approach in the future.

appendix

Outside Help — Advantages and Snags

Many people have a particular nightmare that frightens and disturbs them more than anything else. For children it is often great slime-encrusted monsters, and for managers it is often consultants.

Many managers see consultants as a special kind of vermin who dash into an organization, rapidly come to only a partial understanding of the problem, and then make recommendations that are either callous, irrelevant, or cripplingly expensive.

But although there are many hazards in using outside help, sometimes it is absolutely essential if you are to get things moving. And, believe it or not, there is a new breed of consultant and adviser who has learned to be genuinely helpful and who is rapidly replacing the stop-watch-clicking, high-pressure, encyclopedia-salesman type of yesteryear.

Choosing appropriate outside help, however, is far from easy. Care, concern, and a bit of wariness are essential.

FORMS OF OUTSIDE HELP

Help comes in two basic forms: either it can come to you or you can go to it.

Help that comes to you and deals with your specific problems is called *consultancy*. Consultancy is generally useful when a problem is far too complex or specialized for your own people to handle or when it is concerned with challenging the accepted values, principles, traditions, and habitual patterns of the organization.

There are two basic styles in which consultants operate. First, there are those who come in, solve the problem, give you the solution, and then go away. The drawback to this approach is that, although the problem is solved, in the short term your own management team will not be any better equipped the next time a similar problem occurs. This is the kind of consultancy style that is fine if, for instance, you have an infrequent job for which it is more convenient and efficient to subcontract a specialist than to acquire the necessary skills in your organization.

However, it is a different situation if your problem is one that you ought to learn to solve for yourself. Say, for example, you are expanding rapidly and feel that your management team is either poorly organized or not developing as fast as your expansion demands. These kinds of problems are fundamental to the life of the organization, and it is simply not appropriate to subcontract them to an outsider. If you do, the chances are that your people will feel resentful and uncommitted to the solution.

Nevertheless, a consultant may be needed to help you begin working on a problem. In this case, his job is to help you work on your own problems, to help you organize the work you are doing, to help you learn from the experience, and perhaps to challenge some of your accepted practices. This kind of consultancy is often referred to as *process consultancy*, and it demands a special kind of consultant who will concentrate on helping you work more effectively on your own problems.

Therefore, when you have a problem that looks as though it needs a consultant, it is important to ask whether you need to work on the problem yourself in order to be able eventually to tackle that kind of issue in the future.

Choosing a Consultant

If you do decide to use a consultant and are not really accustomed to this kind of help, it is likely that you will find the selection process quite discomfiting. However, each of us in this situation must learn, for himself, how to choose helpers.

Consultants can be extremely helpful in the "people-development" area of an organization. Unfortunately, you need someone who can be trusted and accepted by both managers and staff, and such a consultant is not easy to find.

In a large organization, there are often people at hand who can act as internal consultants. It may also be possible to establish a link with a local management college or training association. If this is not possible, however, you can turn to the commercial consultant.

The main difficulty with a commercial consultant is finding the right one. We have found that the best consultants for us are not the polished and pompous, but rather those who listen, clarify objectives, and deal quietly and effectively with our particular needs. The consultant who feels like a gritty object in a glass of scotch will be trouble-some and will muddle an already difficult situation.

Generally, consultants tend to be bright, persuasive, authoritarian, and overwhelming. This does not, however, guarantee that they will suit your needs. Consultants are neither omniscient nor indispensable. Do not commit yourself to hiring one, or be pressured into signing a contract, unless the consultant is one with whom you would like to work—and only then when *you* feel ready.

Shotgun marriages are more likely to lead to unhappiness and divorce than the gradual ritual of courtship and engagement—and so it is with consultants. Take your time and interview a few. You can invite those you "warm up to" to handle some limited work.

There are many first-rate consultants around, but there are also others who can easily seduce you into signing expensive contracts or paying an astronomical daily rate that suggests they are worth three times more than you. To avoid being disappointed or "ripped off," we suggest you ask the following questions before working with a consultant.

1. Does the consultant have the time to do a proper job?
2. Is he trying to help you or sell himself? (Whose interests does he serve—yours or his?)
3. Do you trust him as a professional?
4. Is he more interested in supporting your efforts or undermining them?
5. Does he really want to understand you and your situation?

If the answer is "yes" to each of these questions, try the consultant on a limited basis.

To be able to respond adequately to the consultant's suggestions and to put matters in perspective, try to get an overall "feel" of the scale of action required in your situation. Then, as the consultant tackles your problems, see whether a relationship of trust can be developed, investigate whether people value his contribution, and ask if, as a result of his efforts, any improvements have been noted and appreciated.

Other Forms of Help

The other primary sources of help that you can approach easily are in the form of external training courses, workshops, seminars, and management texts and theories. Although much time, effort, and money have been wasted on these forms of training in recent years, we often underestimate the benefits that can be derived from them.

All of us need to learn and grow continuously to avoid becoming narrow-minded and crystallized. But learning and growing need to be managed consciously like any other resource; otherwise, they can easily become a ritual or a hedge to facing problems. Training courses often bring insight, management theories create their own "ideal" solutions, but, without action, combined with responsibility and sound judgment, all new insights lead to anxiety and frustration.

Management must take the final responsibility to make an organization work—this must be kept as a sacred principle. As Abraham Lincoln once said, "You cannot help men permanently by doing for them what they should do for themselves."

Although the world is full of consultants, training courses, and authors who would have you believe that their approach, course, seminar, or book is just what you need, we believe that learning is best achieved by practical exploration, experimentation, and achievement. The risks may seem great, but the resulting benefits will add much to your personal and organizational growth and development.

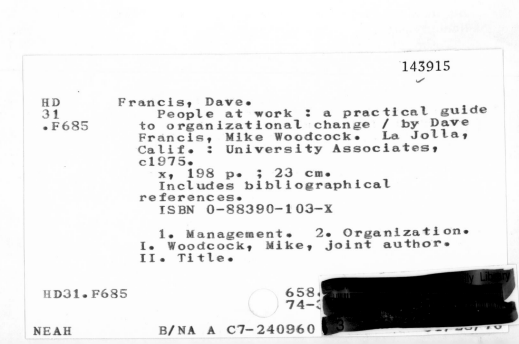